Witchcraft,
Mysticism
and Magic
in the
Black World

OTHER BOOKS BY JAMES HASKINS

Diary of a Harlem Schoolteacher

Resistance: Profiles in Nonviolence

Revolutionaries: Agents of Change

The War and the Protest: Vietnam

Profiles in Black Power

A Piece of the Power: Four Black Mayors

From Lew Alcindor to Kareem Abdul Jabbar

Religions

The Psychology of Black Language,
  with Hugh F. Butts, M.D.

Black Manifesto for Education—Editor

Jokes From Black Folks

Pinckney Benton Stewart Pinchback: A Biography

Adam Clayton Powell: Portrait of a Marching Black

Street Gangs: Yesterday and Today

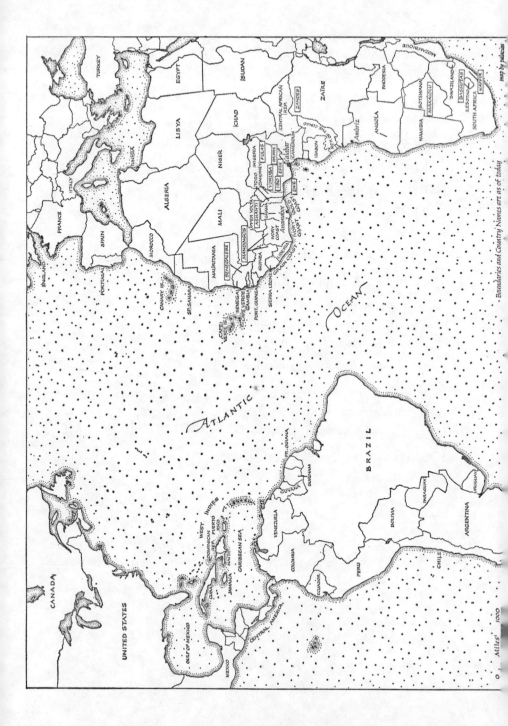

Boundaries and Country Names are as of today.

maps by palacios

Miles 0 1000

Witchcraft, Mysticism and Magic in the Black World

James Haskins

Doubleday & Company, Inc.
Garden City, New York

ENDPAPERS: photograph by Lisa Little is of the figure of a Royal Ancestor, carved in wood, from Bangwa Tribe, Cameroon. It is part of the collection of the Museum of Primitive Art, New York.

ISBN: 0-385-02878-4 Trade
     0-385-09657-7 Prebound
Library of Congress Catalog Card Number 73-11708

TO GRANDMA HATTIE, who first got me started with her tales from her childhood about witchcraft and voodoo.

GRATEFUL ACKNOWLEDGMENT is due to my editor, Pat Connolly, for her faith and her help, to Ruth Ann Stewart and Ann Kalkhoff for their help in gathering the material for the book, and to Mary Ellen Arrington for typing the manuscript. A special thanks to Kathy Benson, without whom this book would not have been possible.

Contents

Chapter 1

The New
Wave of
Mysticism

And the Old

In Louisville, Kentucky, a young army officer and his wife welcome a small group of people to their comfortable split-level home. The guests, dressed neatly but casually, include a computer programmer, a store clerk, and a psychology major from the University of Louisville. They are led downstairs to a wood-paneled recreation room with a vinyl floor—a room very much like thousands of other recreation rooms in middle-class homes across the country.

Except that at one end of this recreation room is a black-draped altar, and next to it, on the wall, is a chartreuse green goat image in a purple star. The people look like millions of other middle-class people across the country—except that they are at this house not to party or drink beer or watch a basketball game but to worship Satan.

In southern New Jersey a thirty-year-old receptionist winds thread around a voodoo doll and sticks pins into it in a serious effort to make another woman in the office resign.

In San Francisco a three-story, solid black structure has been erected. It is the headquarters of the First Church of Satan; the head of the First Church of Satan, Anton LaVey, lives here and presides over a nationwide congregation claimed to be over ten thousand members. LaVey practices black magic and, to his great delight, is called "America's black pope." In San Francisco and in other parts of California, police report that youths are found carrying fetish bags that contain drugs, potions, animal bones, and occasionally human fingers.

In Washington, D.C., Jeane Dixon, a clairvoyant or foreteller of the future, has as clients some of the most important names in business, politics and show business.

In New York City's Washington Square Park two New York University students decide to find out who stole one of their library books. They capture a lizard, put it under a magic spell devised by the Hopi Indians of the Southwest and ask it the name of the thief. Although they are supposedly bright young men, they fully believe that the lizard will then speak, in a very small voice, and reveal the identity of the thief.

Similar and stranger things are happening across the country, in cities and towns, among young and old, wealthy and poor, educated and uneducated. A wave of mysticism has hit America and, to a lesser extent, Europe. It began a few years ago with a revival of interest in astrology. Astrologists started appearing on television and radio to discuss the astrological charts of famous people or to make forecasts for the future based on their calculations of the movements of the sun, moon and planets. Paperbacks devoted to each astrological sign began to appear in bookstores and on drugstore bookracks. The song from the Broadway musical *Hair* entitled "The Age of Aquarius" became a hit single. People had their astrological charts drawn up by writing to any number of mail order houses. Computer dating services promised to match their customers with people of compatible signs. Today, when two people meet, often the first question is not "What do you do?" or "Where do you live?" but "What sign are you?"

Interest in astrology expanded into interest in extrasensory perception (ESP) and parapsychology, Ouija boards and tarot-card reading. Within the past two or three years, witchcraft has come to the fore in both its "white" and "black" forms. "White" witchcraft is the tamer form, emphasizing that good and evil are repaid three times within one's lifetime and that ritual and ceremony are used to help, heal and pay homage to the ancient gods and goddesses. "Black" witchcraft can be violent and cruel. It stresses the idea that there is a demon inside all men and that it can be exorcised only by being channeled into ritualized hatred. In between these two forms is every shade of gray imaginable, forms that blend both "white" and "black" witchcraft in varying degrees.

With the growing popularity of witchcraft came the appearance of Satanism. The 1968 movie *Rosemary's Baby* probably did more to publicize Satanism than did any of the small but growing cults of Satan that existed at that time. Since then other, similar movies have been produced, and the cults of Satan are now popular enough not to need much publicizing. Although such religious movements as the Jesus Freaks and the Children of God have received much newspaper and magazine coverage in the past few years, they have not attracted anything like the numbers of young people who have joined witches' covens or satanic cults.

Witchcraft, mysticism and magic have always held a strong fascination for mankind. Folklore abounds with mystical and magical elements, as does the history of religion. With the great age of scientific discovery in Europe, during the fourteenth, fifteenth, and sixteenth centuries, many of the questions and mysteries that man had previously turned to witchcraft, mysticism and magic to solve were answered by science. And as a consequence belief and practice in these three areas declined. Yet they have enjoyed a resurgence at various periods of history since then. These have been periods of great social upheaval, like our own time, when science, rationalism and religion have just not been enough.

What needs does this wave of witchcraft, mysticism, and magic satisfy? One is a great desire for rituals, for ordered, disciplined, strictly defined actions. Americans today enjoy so much freedom that they are threatened by it. In just about every area of life the atmosphere is one of "anything goes." A person can dress the way he wants, hold a job or not, go to church or not, be polite to others or not, "do his own thing." The problem for many is that they do not know what "their own thing" is, and they would prefer having some rules to follow, some goals set for them, some codes established. Without such things they feel lost, lacking a sense of self or a sense of belonging. John Godwin studied the various occult movements in America today and noticed the great importance that rituals enjoyed in each of them:

At first I was mildly astonished over the accent placed on lengthy—and to me rather pointless— ceremonials in the various cult organizations. Much of the literature germinated by them contains little else but endless ritualistic pageantry that has to be learned by heart and executed correctly down to the minutest detail. I soon learned that for many members these are the most important and satisfying aspects of the creed, that by performing them they achieve a sense of belonging, of worth, that no other function can fully re-replace.[1]

The current wave of witchcraft, mysticism and magic also satisfies the need for answers to and understanding of the many frustrating aspects of the world in the twentieth century. Why can't people of different races get along together? Why are our cities so sick? With all our knowledge and resources, why is there still hunger? Why have so many people lost their basic respect for others? For many, occult movements offer certain universal truths and ways of appealing to these truths. They offer a belief that life and the human condition could be perfect if only human beings would understand the path to perfection.

One of the most striking things about the current occult revival is that it is predominantly a white phenomenon. Blacks can be found in the membership of the various cults—a college student here, a middle-class matron there—and there are a few black mystics with an integrated clientele, or cults with an integrated membership. But in general blacks are quite noticeably absent. Some will say the reason is that the occult movement is a leisure class movement and that blacks haven't the time or money to devote to it. Others will say that blacks do not have the freedom "problem" that has caused so many whites to turn to the occult. As second-class citizens, blacks do have rules to follow and codes of behavior set for them if only by the harshness and difficulty of their lives. But the chief reason for the absence of black participation in this *new* wave of occultism is that witchcraft, mysticism and magic have always been part of the black world; there is no need to participate in a new wave when the old wave is still strong.

The supernatural theme has always been strong in the black experience. It has not known the ups and downs of popularity and interest that have characterized the white world's opinion of mysticism and magic; it has never been a "fad." The conditions of slavery and second-class citizenship have helped to make witchcraft, mysticism and magic consistently powerful forces among blacks, for they offer means of spiritual escape from degrading life situations. But the black world of the supernatural is not made less legitimate because of the sociological and psychological factors that have nurtured it in the past. In fact, its remarkable staying power and consistency, compared to the white world of witchcraft, mysticism and magic, make it, in many ways, more legitimate than its white counterpart. Also, the conditions of slavery and second-class citizenship, although they have been in large measure responsible for the staying power of the supernatural in the black experience, were by no means the reasons why witchcraft, mysticism and magic *became* part of that experience. In this book it will be shown that many supernatural beliefs and practices among blacks are directly traceable to African beliefs and practices, and that the main reason why the supernatural is such an important part of everyday black life today is that it was an even more important part of everyday African life.

Although there are similarities between the black supernatural world and the white supernatural world, there are many differences. The chief similarity, of course, is the fact of belief itself. In both worlds, belief in the supernatural exists out of the human need to believe in something higher or more powerful than oneself. Another similarity is the idea that a higher being has the power to help mankind or the individual if properly worshiped. The differences lie primarily in the means of worship. Among whites, worship usually takes place in groups—at Black Masses, at séances, at ceremonies to Satan. Among blacks, except in voodoo, where there are some group rituals, worship is primarily an individual thing. This custom began during slavery, when slaves were forbidden to meet together in groups, and it has persisted to the present day. Among whites, the occult is practiced at certain defined times, chiefly when a meeting or service is held. When members of cults are not at meetings, their belief is not expressed in their daily routine to any great extent. Among blacks, the occult is part of the daily routine. When the front stoop is washed, it is not simply washed for purposes of cleanliness; it is washed to ward off evil spirits. When an object cannot be found, it is not just considered misplaced, it is quickly searched for and if not found is assumed to have been stolen by an enemy for an evil purpose. Among blacks Satan or the Devil is not a personification of evil or of the demon in man; he is almost a comic figure, a scapegoat for human failings and errors. Blacks would not think of worshiping the Devil in the way that the white cults of Satan do, for blacks know that there is bad in man as well as good, and they do not celebrate the bad any more than they celebrate the good.

Before we go on, it is necessary to point out that when the terms *black experience* or *black world* or *black community* or even *blacks* are used, they are used in a general sense. Just as not all whites believe in or practice witchcraft, mysticism and magic, neither do all blacks. But there is a separate, fascinating black world of witchcraft, mysticism and magic that should be made known in this time of rebirth of interest in the supernatural.

Chapter 2

The
Roots
in
Africa

The home of black witchcraft, mysticism and magic is, of course, the home of black people—Africa. Although a study of mystical and magical practices in modern Africa would be fascinating, our purpose here is to look at those beliefs and practices that existed in Africa at the time of the slave trade, in the sixteenth, seventeenth and eighteenth centuries. We will also look mainly at the beliefs and practices of the parts of Africa from which most of the slaves were taken, for it was these beliefs and practices that were brought with the slaves to the New World.

The majority of the people who were brought to the New World as slaves were West Africans. All the major slave ports were on the west coast of Africa; ports on the eastern and southern coasts were rare. Some historians have believed that large slaving parties went into the African interior to bring back slaves on thousand-mile marches to the western coast, but few, if any, such marches took place. Geographical hazards and the danger of encountering hostile tribes, not to mention the practical problems of transporting a large number of captives for a thousand miles, would have made such expeditions unprofitable. In addition, there are the slave traders' documents of the period, which often tell the various places of origin of the slaves. The vast majority were from West Africa, from the nations of Dahomey and Togo, from the Ashanti and Igbo tribes, and many more.

The West African nations to which the European slavers came in the eighteenth century, when the greatest numbers of slaves were shipped to the New World, had highly developed civilizations, with strong systems of government, usually based on kinship. They had systems of census-taking and taxation. They were economically sophisticated, with highly developed art forms and very strong systems of religion, which incorporated supernatural and magical beliefs and practices. It is these systems that concern us here.

First, it is necessary to point out that, in Africa even today, religion and magic are not separated as they are in Europe and America. In fact, in Africa, many things that we would consider opposites are seen as simply two sides of the same coin. More examples of this viewpoint will be given later. For now, we will try to consider African *religion* and African *magical practices* separately as much as possible, in order that they may be more easily understood. But there really is no line that can be drawn between the two.

AFRICAN RELIGION

Just as no line could be drawn to separate the religious practices of the West African nations, from which the greatest number of slaves came, no line could be drawn between religious and nonreligious life. West African religion was not removed from life, not something thought about only on Sundays or only in the morning and at night. It was deeply entwined in nearly every part of daily life. The forces of the universe, whether good or bad, were always close at hand, to be appealed to in time of doubt or fear, to be consulted when important steps were to be taken, and to be appealed to when help was needed. Religion was, first and foremost, between the individual and the spirits he worshiped. And thus in West Africa religion was very informal—and very simple to understand and very ritualistic.

The West Africans worshiped many gods and

spirits, particularly those associated with natural objects. The sun, for instance, was worshiped as all-powerful and all-knowing. River spirits were very important, as were thunder gods; so were various living creatures, among them the snake. In the nation of Dahomey the serpent-god Dan was worshiped as a god of good fortune; his color was white. In Dahomey there were also worshiped two rainbow serpents, Aido Hwedo and Damballa Hwedo. They were believed to have been present at the creation of the world. Certain locations were inhabited by important gods. There was always a god who guarded the entrances to villages, households and sacred shrines. In Dahomey he was called Legba; in Yoruba country he was called Elegbara. There were gods of the crossroads and gods of the fields and gods of the mountains and gods of the forests. There were gods everywhere, and this was natural for a people to whom religion was an essential part of everyday life.

What distinguished African society from other societies in which religion was equally important in everyday life was its willingness to accept new gods. Basically, the idea was that if a god was effective he should be worshiped, no matter whose god he was originally. If worship of this god brought some good to the worshiper, then he was adopted. He could even make a few mistakes; after all, no one was perfect. If one tribe conquered another, the conquered tribe readily adopted the gods of the conquerors. The very fact that the conquerors had won meant that their gods must be more powerful. Throughout the centuries, wars among the various tribes had caused certain gods to become widely worshiped.

In addition to these universal gods, who could be claimed by all, each clan, and thus each person, worshiped ancestors. Ancestral cults were extremely important in West African societies, and, as an elaborate family or kinship system, they formed the strongest basis of government. West Africans believed that the power of a man did not end with death; he simply moved to another plane of existence from which he watched over his descendants. Distinctions among different classes of people continued on this different plane of existence. Ancestors of royal or chieftains' families enjoyed more power than farmers' ancestors. In some societies, among them Dahomey and the society of the Yoruba, in what is now Nigeria, ancestors were actually considered gods.

Ancestors were believed not only to watch over their descendants but to intervene in their lives—if they were properly honored. Thus it was very important to ensure ancestral good will by honoring the dead with long and costly rituals. The funeral was seen as the true climax of life. A person's funeral had to be in keeping with his position in the community if he was to take his rightful place in the afterworld. Surviving relatives were moved to provide this proper funeral for two reasons. One was that providing a proper funeral would not only enhance their prestige in the eyes of the community but also assure concern for them on the part of their ancestors. The other was that if they did not provide a proper funeral they believed the resentment of the neglected dead person would rebound on the heads of the surviving members of his family. Neglect would make him a fearsome spirit—a discontented, restless, vengeful ghost.

Honoring dead ancestors did not end with the providing of a proper funeral. Individual ancestors and ancestral families were honored in many acts of everyday life as well as in periodic formal ceremonies.

In addition to all these gods and spirits, the West Africans believed in two other forces. One was Fate. The other was what might be called the divine trickster. West Africans believed that Fate ruled the universe. The destiny of each man, everything that happened in his life, was already worked out in a plan. Many Europeans believed in Fate too, but Europeans believed there was no way to escape the plan Fate had for them. Africans did believe there was a way out—through the divine trickster.

Actually, the divine trickster was more a concept than a single god, for the divine trickster could take several forms. He could be the youngest child of a particular god; he could be the most recent ancestor to die and enter the afterworld; he could also be a certain god who seemed especially to symbolize the idea that good and bad were not really all that separate.

The youngest child of a particular god was the one who carried the message of the god to the various divine families as to what was in store for a man. But as he was a trickster he could be persuaded by the man to change the orders he carried. Thus, if some bad event was due in the man's life, and the man was a serious worshiper, the trickster could substitute a good fate for the bad fate, or vice versa.

Legba, or Elegbara, was originally the god who guarded entrances to villages, houses and shrines. As time went on, Legba was also seen as the god of the crossroads and as the god who "opened the gate" for the other gods at all rituals. He was an example of an established god who was basically seen as a trickster. He was worshiped by all no matter what cults they belonged to, because, as the messenger of the gods, he was the one to be approached first with a request to the gods; he also had the power to set aside bad fates in the destiny of a person or to make bad fates worse, or to change good fates into bad fates. In other words, different tricksters had different powers. The youngest child of a god worshiped by a particular cult carried messages back and forth between the god and the worshipers of the god, and thus he had the power to change these messages or to hasten or slow their progress. Legba, the messenger of all the gods and worshiped by all persons, could change many more messages and many more worshipers' lives.

When Christian missionaries arrived in Africa to spread Christianity, they often identified Legba as the Devil. One reason why they did so was that, more than any other African god, Legba symbolized the West African idea that good and bad were not distinct. The missionaries could not understand this idea, and thus they could not understand the Africans to whom they were trying to carry Christianity.

Unlike Europeans, who tended to see life in terms of good or bad, black or white, Africans understood that there was really no absolute good or absolute evil and that both good and evil resided in everything. Nothing was so good that it could not cause inconvenience to someone; nothing was so bad that someone somewhere could not benefit from it. In many ways, this complete realism would help those Africans who were brought to the New World, to survive slavery. But this will be treated in the next chapter.

Means of worship were as various as the gods who were worshiped. Individual persons could honor their ancestors or their particular gods in many acts of their daily lives and in many of their daily thoughts. But most individuals also belonged to organized groups, or cults, in which they engaged in worship with other individuals. Sometimes the organized group was a family; sometimes it was a community. Sometimes its rituals, or means of worship, were very carefully defined; sometimes they were improvised.

Most river cults, for example, had clearly defined rituals. A widespread ritual involved a visit to a sacred river or to some other body of "living" water, such as the ocean, to obtain the liquid essential for the rites. This might involve quite a long journey to the particular sacred stream. Once, in the West African country of Dahomey, the bed of a sacred stream that had run dry was filled from nearby wells so that this water could be drawn from the same traditional place.

Periodically, pilgrimages were made to sacred bodies of water, and it was during these pilgrimages that the highest form of worship of the water spirits would occur, and the water spirits would reward their worshipers by becoming visible to them. The spirit would "enter the head" of a worshiper and would cause him to fling himself into the water. He would no longer have control of his own actions; he would be "possessed."

In any cult, whether it was a cult of river spirits or a snake cult or an ancestral cult, although the chief means of worship were music and dance, the highest form of worship was possession. When a worshiper became "possessed" by a spirit or a deity, he was "chosen" by that spirit or deity and for a brief time he merged with it. He lost control of his own actions and, in a way, *became* the spirit or deity, remembering nothing of the experience after it was over. An outsider observing such a possession might see it as hysterical, but in reality possession took definite, controlled forms. For one thing, not everyone could be possessed, and possession could only take place during actual religious ceremonies. If, during a ceremony, a worshiper had been feeling an unexplained restlessness or the priest chose a particular worshiper, these two could experience possession.

In the river cults, the ceremony and the possession usually occurred around a body of water into which the possessed leaped. But in most other cults the ceremony occurred on land, with all the worshipers dancing, counterclockwise, in a circle. The one to be possessed began by clapping his hands, nodding his head, and tapping his feet in time to the rhythm of the drums, like the others. But soon, the one to be possessed was easily distinguished from the others. His gaze became fixed, his eyes became glassy. His movements became faster and faster. His head was thrown back; his arms thrashed about. Then he ran into the center of the circle, and there he gave way to his god in every way imaginable. He fell on the ground, jumped up and down, rolled around, whirled around, spoke "in tongues," saying words he had never heard before. Meanwhile, the other worshipers moved around in a circle about him, always in a counterclockwise direction, and the drums beat to the rhythm of the possessed. Sometimes he danced and whirled and spoke in tongues until he fainted with exhaustion. Sometimes he felt the spirit gradually leave him, and as he descended to the plane of the other dancers he rejoined the circle. Always the drummers continued to beat the rhythm of the god until all the worshipers had returned to complete knowledge of who they were or where they were. If the drums stopped before this point, there was the danger that their own spirits would not return to them.

Possession, by the way, is not just an African, or black, experience. It is also a European experience. The major difference is that in Europe possession always comes to a person when he is alone—he experiences a miracle or a revelation. In Africa, possession always comes to a person when he is with others.

Possession could not occur unless it occurred in an organized group. And an organized group could not meet unless it was led by a priest. The priest knew the correct ways to worship the particular deity —what songs to sing, what dances to dance, what charms to employ. It was the priest who led the pilgrimages and who designated which worshipers were to be possessed. Often young people went through considerable training in order to become priests, sometimes being segregated from others during the training process. Priests enjoyed a very favored role in African society.

AFRICAN MAGIC

In our society, which is Western society, religion and magic, religion and mysticism, religion and belief in the supernatural are separated. In Africa, they were not. Although Americans and Europeans certainly did practice witchcraft and mysticism, they did not believe such practices would affect God. In fact, most religious Americans and Europeans believed such practices to be *against* religion and *against* God. Africans believed that magic and witchcraft were powerful ways to affect their spirits and gods, as well as to affect each other.

Of course, in Africa, magic was used for everyday personal purposes, just as it was used in Europe and America. But the fact that it was used for religious purposes as well—in fact came into every aspect of daily life—has caused outsiders to label African religion "fetishism." A fetish is, most simply, a charm, and African life abounds in charms. But just the brief treatment of African religion in the preceding pages should have shown that there is much more to African religion than just the use of charms.

Anyway, charms were very important and very numerous. Everyone wore charms around their ankles, around their wrists, about their necks, or they suspended charms from the roofs of their houses or inserted them in carved figurines or placed them in their shrines. The charms were often made of materials such as colored cloth, white clay, spines, strong hairs and pointed objects. The idea of "like to like" was followed whenever possible. Sacred water was used in the worship of river spirits, snakeskins in the worship of snakes. The charms were used to protect a person from an enemy, or to hurt an enemy; as a protection against disease or to inflict a disease upon another. To cause another to love one, or to follow one's wishes. To influence a god or spirit to be benevolent, to influence a god or spirit to change a bad fate to a good fate. The powers of the charms were as numerous as the charms themselves—in fact, more numerous. For many charms had more than one use. A charm that was used to protect its owner could also bring harm to an attacker. For example, a charm to cure smallpox in its owner could also be used to give smallpox to an enemy. For like a coin, a charm had two sides. Here again, we find the African idea that good and bad are not clearly separated.

In addition to the charms that were made of powdered bones and hair, there were charms that were carved of wood to look like people or animals. Artists of the Ashanti tribe (in what is now Ghana) made carvings chiefly of fairies and forest monsters. The most striking feature of these carved fairies, which the Ashanti called *mmoatia*, was their feet, which always pointed backwards. Usually the figures were about a foot tall and painted red, black or white. They were believed to communicate with each other by whistling. They represented real fairies who were invisible. The black fairies were more or less harmless, but the white and red "little people" were always up to some sort of mischief, stealing housewives' palm wine or the food left over from previous meals.

The forest monsters, or Sasabonsam, in which the Ashanti also believed were said to be covered with long hair, to have large bloodshot eyes, to have long legs and feet pointing both ways. They sat on high tree branches and dangled their legs, and when unwary hunters passed by the Sasabonsam wrapped their legs around them and they were trapped. Hunters who went into the forest and were never heard from again were thought to have been caught by the Sasabonsam. The forest monsters were believed to be hostile to man and particularly to priests, but sometimes they were supposed to add power to positive charms. This shows again the African belief that even in the worst things some good can be found.

In Dahomey and among the Yoruba there was also a belief in "little people." The fairies were believed to live in a number of different places; those in the forests were said to approach hunters and to give them knowledge of medicines and of magic that made those men who were hunters so powerful. In Dahomey, there was a belief in forest monsters similar to those believed in by the Ashanti. The Dahomean forest monsters were supposed to be fire-breathing and many-horned and to attack unsuspecting hunters. Dahomean hunters, however, seemed luckier than Ashanti warriors in escaping these monsters. Often, they were able to climb a tree and call their dogs to fight off the attacker.

The "little folk" were also a part of African daily life. Like Irish gremlins, they were blamed for minor accidents and misplaced objects. They were a recognized part of every household, even though they were invisible, and although they could do bad deeds, they could do good deeds as well.

Even though so many things in African magic

were both good and bad, depending upon the situation, some general distinctions were made between good and bad. One such distinction was made between practitioners of good magic and practitioners of bad magic. There were "medicine men" and there were "conjurers."

Medicine men usually practiced "good" magic. Not only did they make healing medicines of plants and herbs and minerals, but also they gave advice to those who came to them—advice on how to protect oneself against evil forces, how to prosper, how to gain good fortune. Medicine men were rarely hated or feared by the community.

The conjurer, or witch doctor, used his knowledge and his powers more often for harmful than for beneficial purposes. He was sought out by those who wished to harm or destroy others. However, and here the idea of good and bad as two sides of the same coin comes in again, since it was possible for bad magic to be turned back against the one who desired to use it for his own purposes, the conjurer was hated and feared. He was usually blamed for whatever went wrong in a village, and sometimes conjurers were driven from the village, if not hunted down and killed.

West Africans also believed in witches, ghosts and vampires, and it is in this belief that we find the closest similarity between African and European magic. In West Africa, as in Europe, the majority of witches were believed to be women, and not necessarily old women. If an old witch wanted her daughter to become a witch, she simply bathed her daughter repeatedly with "medicine." A witch's greatest desire was to eat people, but she never did so outright. Rather, she sucked blood. Each witch favored a different part of the body, and when she visited her victim at night she would suck all the blood from the particular part of the body of which she was fond. In the morning the victim would awake complaining of illness and die before nightfall.

Witches always tried to obtain some object that belonged to the intended victim—hair, nail cuttings, waist beads. Names were used in much the same way by the witches, and in West Africa names were of great importance. At birth a child was given a name by a particular relative. This was his "real" name, and the identification of this "real" name with the personality of the bearer was believed so complete that it had to be kept secret lest it come into the hands of someone who might use it in working evil magic against him. At other periods of the person's life, different names would be given him. These periods were not only those that were marked by rites as new stages in his development, such as puberty and marriage, but also those times when something very important happened to the person. A witch could know these names but would be able to do little magic with them; but much magic could be worked with a "real" name.

Witches could transform themselves into birds, especially owls, crows, vultures and parrots, into houseflies and fireflies, and into such animals as hyenas, leopards, lions, elephants and snakes.

Naturally, there were methods to catch, hold and punish witches. Witches were believed to leave behind their skin when they went out, and thus the most common antiwitch method was to sprinkle salt and pepper on her skin, which would prevent her from getting back into it. A more general antiwitchcraft method was to keep a frizzled hen in the yard, for she would scratch up and destroy all conjuration.

Superstitions and minor rituals abounded in West Africa, and they governed nearly every action of a person, no matter how minor or how important. Many surrounded the birth and early years of a child. West Africans believed that the soul or spirit of a person was not terribly "loyal" and that throughout life a human being had to exercise special care in order to "hold on" to his soul lest it leave him. Naturally, an infant or a small child would not have as strong a hold on his soul as an adult would, and many practices centered upon helping the child to keep his soul. When a journey was planned on which the child would be taken, the child's soul was always "called," and it was called again at every crossroads. Otherwise, the spirit might get left behind. Another ritual marked the appearance of permanent teeth. A rite was performed with the first baby tooth to come out, in order that the permanent teeth would come in strong and beautiful. In Dahomey this tooth was tossed onto the roof of the mother's house. Old people, who were losing their teeth, saved them, as they saved their hair clippings and nail parings, in order that when they went to the grave they would do so "whole," with everything that belonged to them.

Daily rituals included casting food and drink from the meal upon the floor so that the little people might have their share. Usually, persons believed they were descended from a particular animal or plant, and this they would not eat, believing that to do so would bring on illness, especially skin eruptions. A certain day of the week would see no one working in the fields. In Dahomey that day was Mioxi. It was believed that if a person worked in the fields on Mioxi he would incur the wrath of the thunder gods and be struck dead by lightning. And to this day in the North American South, it is the custom among blacks to unplug electrical appliances during a thunderstorm, and to sit still and in silence, because "God is doing his work," and such times are dangerous to mankind. When to work, what to eat, when to choose a name—so many actions were governed by the gods and by a sense of closeness to the supernatural.

These, then, were the major aspects of West African religion and magic when European slave traders began to conduct their inhuman but extremely profitable business in the sixteenth century. These customs were carried with the slaves to the New World, where they continued but, under new situations and in new environments, changed.

Chapter 3

Witchcraft, Mysticism and Magic in Slavery Times

"They came in chains," Saunders Redding wrote in his book of the same title, "and they came from everywhere along the west coast of Africa—from Cape Verde and the Bights of Benin and Biafra; from Goree, Gambia, and Calabar; Anamaboe and Ambriz; the Gold, the Ivory, and the Grain Coast; and from a thousand villages inland. They were, these slaves, people of at least four great races— the Negritians, the Fellatahs, the Bantus and the

Gallas—and many tribes whose names make a kind of poetry: Makalolu, Bassutas, Kaffir, Koromantis; the Senegalese and the Mandingos; Ibos, Iboni, Ibani (like the parsing of a Latin verb), Efik and Fulahs, the Wysyahs and the Zandes."[2]

They were bound in chains—warriors, priests, farmers, men, women and children. They were uprooted from their land, taken away from their families and communities, stolen from their religion and their culture. They were carried to an alien land inhabited by strange and cruel people, who spoke a language they could not understand. And if all this were not nightmare enough, the African slaves could not even find comfort in each other.

They were from many different tribes, spoke many different languages, held many different beliefs. Trying to communicate was like an Italian, a Frenchman, a Chinese and an American trying to communicate. Trying to hold religious ceremonies together was like a Catholic, a Buddhist, a Hindu and a Jew trying to hold religious ceremonies together. Their only common bond was their slavery, their sorrow and their pain.

But though the slaves represented many different tribes, a majority were from three or four nations and tribes—Dahomey, Togo, Ashanti and Igbo. In any small group of slaves there was likely to be at least one slave from one of these nations. In any large group of slaves there were likely to be more. Thus, as time went on, slaves from these nations began to impose their language, beliefs and customs upon the others, or, rather, slaves from other nations began to adopt the language, beliefs, and customs of these three or four nations. The slaves' need was to communicate with each other, and naturally they learned the languages that the majority of slaves spoke, and learned the rituals and practices in which the greatest number of slaves believed. Eventually, there were not enough of the minority tribes on a plantation to take part in their traditional customs and dances, or even to carry on the language. Children growing up heard another African language far more often than their own, learned other African religious beliefs and magical practices which seemed far better than their own. Thus it was the religion and magic of these three or four nations that survived best in the New World.

Even the religion and magic of these three or four nations would not have survived as well as they did in the New World if religious priests, medicine men and conjurers had not been here to direct the religious and magical practices and rituals. It is the mistaken belief of some people that the slaves who were brought to the New World came from the most undesirable classes of Africans, that the royalty, the intellectuals and the priests had the power to escape kidnaping. This was not the case at all.

According to tradition, in Dahomey, many persons of the royal class were enslaved as a result of dynastic quarrels. If two brothers, for example, disputed each other's right to the throne, a convenient way for one to dispose of the other was to sell him into slavery. Not only the opponent was sold. After all, he would have had many loyal followers, and, to prevent them from avenging his banishment, the victor would have to sell into slavery also his family and supporting chiefs, his diviners and the priests who advised and aided him. It is historical fact that a Dahomean king, Glele, suffered this sort of fate. Although Glele himself was merely held prisoner by his uncle and not sold into slavery, the queen mother and a number of others in the royal court were sold. Years later, after he had regained the throne, Glele sent an emissary to Brazil to find and bring back his mother.

Another case was documented in Cuba. A young prince from Luccomees, with several of his nation, had been brought to Cuba and sold to the owner of a plantation. Once on the plantation, for some unknown reason, the young prince was condemned to be flogged. As it was the custom among slave-owners to make an example of wrongdoing, the others were ordered to watch the punishment. But instead of watching, when the prince lay down on the ground to receive his lashes, the others laid themselves down next to him, expressing their loyalty in the desire to share his punishment.[3]

Priests who were not part of royal courts were also sold into slavery as a result of intertribal conflicts. Again, the proof of this has been found in Dahomey. During the eighteenth century the Dahomean nation was expanding, conquering other

West African tribes. Conquering meant imposing its language and religion upon those it conquered. Although the Dahomean policy seems to have been to spare co-operative priests so that the gods of the conquered people would not be made too angry and thus dangerous, priests who refused to co-operate or who were suspected of urging their followers to rebel were quickly sold into slavery. Priests of river cults, especially, suffered this fate. Being the leaders of some of the most powerful cults, they usually refused to submit to the conquerors. It is still a widely held belief in Dahomey today that the reason why the French conquered their country was that the Dahomeans had sold away all the priests who had the power to control the mighty river spirits and that the river gods had revenged this insult by allowing the French to be victorious.

In the early days of slavery in the New World these leaders would have functioned in much the same way as they had functioned in West Africa. Although their activities would have been more limited and would have had to be more secretive under the conditions of slavery, they would have tried to direct the favorable and health-giving forces of nature into the lives of their fellow slaves, who, despite their condition of slavery, still believed in the spirit world and the protecting gods of their homeland.

The presence of priests and medicine men and conjurers among the slaves in the New World would partly explain why there were so many, many revolts

among the slaves in the New World in the early
period of slavery. Their assurance of supernatural
support to both leaders and followers, their promise
that their ancestors were aiding them in their strug-
gle for freedom would have been very important.
They would have given out charms, "gre-gre bags"
or "hands," small parcels containing bits of paper,
bones or potions that hung around the neck or
were carried in some other way for protection or
good luck.

Magic, of course, was a natural support of revolt
and was used often:

Gullah Jack (one of the leaders in Denmark
Vesey's Insurrection in South Carolina in 1822)
was regarded as a sorcerer. . . . He was not only
considered invulnerable, but that he could make
others so by his charms (consisting chiefly of a
crab's claw to be placed in the mouth); and that
he could and certainly would provide all his followers with arms.[4]

In 1712 an insurrection broke out in New York
City which was thought to be related to a school
for young Negroes founded in 1704 by Elias Neau,
an agent for the Society for the Propagation of
the Gospel in Foreign Parts. The plot was actually
brewed by Negroes of the Carmantee and Pappa
tribes of West Africa who, "with the aid of a conjurer, believed that they had made themselves invulnerable."[5]

They would also have helped those many slaves
who chose to commit suicide rather than live without

freedom by instructing them concerning what to do to ensure their return after death to their homeland. A Scandinavian traveler in Cuba told of coming upon eleven slaves who had committed suicide by hanging themselves from the branches of a guasima tree:

They had each one bound his breakfast in a girdle around him; for the African believes that such as die here immediately rise again to new life in their native land. Many female slaves, therefore, will lay upon the corpse of the self-murdered the kerchief, or the head-gear, which she most admires, in the belief that it will thus be conveyed to those who are dear to her in the mother-country, and will bear them a salutation from her. The corpse of a suicide-slave has been seen covered with hundreds of such tokens.[6]

In the early days of slavery the slaves had been allowed a certain amount of freedom to conduct their religious ceremonies and rituals and to beat their drums and dance when they were not working. Such activity was considered harmless by the slaveowners who also felt that freedom to engage in the activities might help their slaves to be more content. As time went on, however, the slaveowners began to realize that these slave activities were not as harmless as they had thought. The slaves had been using the chance to assemble to plan revolts and disturbances. They had been using the drums to send messages. The priests, under the guise of lead-ing religious rituals, had been promising the support of the gods to whatever types of rebellion the slaves desired to engage in. Needless to say, after this discovery on the part of the slaveowners, the slaves were no longer allowed to assemble for religious purposes or to dance. Those recognized as leaders were separated from the rest or sold off the plantations. Such actions were a severe blow to the continuation of traditional organized religious practices among the slaves. Nevertheless, they did continue, despite the fact that other, equally severe threats to the survival of Africanisms were coming in the form of the language, culture, and religions of the slaveowners.

The African slaves who had been brought to the New World had been uprooted from a highly developed society with strong and sophisticated economic, social, artistic, cultural, and religious systems. As time went on, many of their traditions were lost and some were retained. Which were lost and which were retained were a result of the nature of slavery.

For example, the highly developed African economic system was lost entirely. The reason was that slavery itself was an economic system. The function of the slaves was to work, and to work within the system of their masters. Except for what little trading of goods they could conduct among themselves, the elaborate African system of barter in the market place ceased to exist. So did the practice of pawning. Slaves were worked from dawn to dusk, and there was little leisure time for making objects to sell. The fine African art of weaving cloth was lost, as was, for the same reason, the art of wood carving. Such activities required leisure time; a slave did not have leisure time. The African political system was lost among the slaves, especially after slave assemblies were forbidden; there was little opportunity to form groups or to be leaders or followers.

Social institutions managed to survive better. Of course the kinship and clan system suffered. Under slavery it was often difficult to keep even a single family unit together, much less an entire clan. The African tendency to form co-operative groups continued under slavery, chiefly because the slaves were worked in groups. Later, after slavery, mutual benefit societies would be a noticeable characteristic of black communities.

With the recent research into black language we now know that Africanisms have survived in much greater measure than was formerly thought. Of course, as slavery wore on, the slaves began to speak the language of their masters and to forget much of their original languages, even the languages of those three or four nations from whom the majority of slaves had been brought. The reason was communication. Survival required not only that they be able to communicate with each other but also that they be able to communicate with the slave masters. The language of the masters was the language most common to all, and thus the slaves learned to speak a form of the language of their masters which is usually called pidgin. The masters laughed at what seemed a poor and childlike version of their language, forgetting that the slaves did not have the opportunity to learn the new language in school and not realizing that the slaves' original language often "got in the way" just as anyone's native language interferes with his learning a new language. We now know that many aspects of black language, be it black Spanish, English or French, are due not to ignorance but to the persistence of African language forms.

Of all the areas of African society and culture, those of religion and magic enjoyed the greatest survival. One reason was that the slave masters cared less about them. Even when the slave masters had realized the subversive uses the slaves were making of their religious and magical practices, the freedom of the slaves in these areas was always greater than their freedom to work for their own profit or to organize politically. Another was that the slaves themselves clung to these traditions. Religion, magic and the supernatural always enjoy their greatest popularity among a people when the conditions of their earthly lives are hardest to bear. The slaves *had* to believe there was a power or powers to which they could appeal for help; otherwise they would have been unable to go on living.

This is not to say that the slaves did not lose some of their magical and religious practices or that they did not adopt many of the practices of their masters. The African tendency to accept new gods if they seemed to be effective and powerful was a very important influence here. Other important influences were the efforts of Catholic and Protestant missionaries to convert the slaves; in some countries all slaves had to be baptized. Perhaps the most important reason was that the slaves found much in the new religions that they could combine with their traditional beliefs. This was more true of some religions than of others, and more true of a particular religion in a particular country than of the same religion in another country. Magical practices and the attitude toward magic in different countries and regions were also influential.

At this point, it is important to look at slavery in different parts of the New World, for the conditions of slavery and the survival of Africanisms among the slaves in the various countries differ greatly. If the various slaving regions were listed in order of the greatest number of Africanisms to the smallest number, highest on the list would be Surinam (Dutch Guiana) on the northeast coast of South America above Brazil. Next would be the two other Guianas on either side of Surinam, British and French Guiana. Next on the list would be Haiti, in the West Indies, and then the neighboring Santo Domingo (now the Dominican Republic). Next would be the British and Dutch West Indies. Only then would North America appear on the list with the areas of southern Georgia and the South Carolina Sea Islands. Next would come the North American South, and, very last, the North American Northeast, where very few Africanisms managed to survive. New research every day causes this list to be added to or altered, but it will serve as a general outline.

Why the great differences among these areas where African survivals are concerned? The answer has to do with geography and climate, population, ratio of slaves to owners, religion, type of crop, and many other things. In South America, in Brazil and the Guianas, for example, and in the islands of the Caribbean the climate was tropical, much like that of Africa. The slaves brought to these areas thus did not need to adjust to a new climate. These regions were full of jungles and forests and mountains, making escape and safe hiding possible. Certainly the most successful slave revolts occurred in these areas, and not only did the escaped slaves succeed in establishing settlements in the mountains, but also they conducted frequent raids upon isolated plantations to free other slaves. In their mountain hideouts they carried on the African traditions that were their heritage, and thus preserved them.

The plantation system of South America and the Caribbean also favored survival of African traditions. Here the chief crop was sugar, and the plantations were huge, with acres and acres of sugar cane fields. They were owned and operated by wealthy Europeans who had arrived from the Old World already rich and who simply became richer in the New World. Before the importation of African slaves, they had used the native Indians as workers. There was no class of poor whites as there was in the North American South. The sugar plantations required dozens, often hundreds of slaves, and thus on Caribbean and South American plantations, with their population of a few wealthy whites and a huge number of black slaves, the slaves rarely came into contact with anyone but other slaves and some native Indians. This lack of contact meant that the traditions of the slaves were hardly touched by the traditions of their owners. The slaves accepted Christianity on the surface and in private continued their own religious practices. Thus, although in South America and the West Indies, such aspects of African life as their economic and political systems and their artistic traditions were destroyed just as effectively as in other areas, language, religion and magical practices continued practically untouched.

A different situation existed in North America. For one thing, the climate, being temperate, was strange to the slaves. In addition to all the other adjustments that were necessary for them to make, they also had to adjust to different temperatures. The geography was different. There were not the mountain ranges or the dense jungles of South America and the West Indies, and thus in most parts of the North American South there were no invulnerable hideouts for escaped slaves. There were only two areas where good hideouts could be found —the coast of Georgia and the Sea Islands of South Carolina. Both areas contained miles and miles of impassable swamps and small islands, many of which, even today, remain unexplored. The slaves who escaped to these areas made successful escapes, setting up fugitive communities where African traditions were continued, far away from any contact with whites.

In the rest of the South, slave escapes were rarely successful, and as time went on fewer and fewer escapes were attempted.

Although literature on the South in the times of slavery almost always depicts Southern plantations as huge and extending from horizon to horizon, this was not the usual case. Certainly there were some very large plantations, but the majority were quite small, at least in comparison with those in South America and the Caribbean.

In the Deep South of North America the chief crop was cotton, and cotton did not require the large acreage that sugar cane did. Smaller plantations meant fewer slaves. Some had hundreds but more had under fifty. This meant greater contact between slaves and whites, more opportunity for the slaves to learn white ways, less opportunity for the slaves to continue their African traditions. In fact, contact between slaves and whites in the United States was greater in degree than anywhere else in the New World.

In the North American Southeast, in the Virginias and the Carolinas, tobacco was the chief crop. Tobacco did not require large plantations either, and here too there was great contact between slaves and slaveowners. In this area, also, there were urban centers, which hardly existed in South America and the West Indies and which existed only in small numbers in the rest of the North American South. Urbanization is a great equalizer for all groups; the conditions of urban life work against any one group of people carrying on a way of life radically different from that of other groups. Urbanization also worked against the retention of Africanisms.

Of course it was in the North American Northeast that the greatest number of urban centers existed, and that is one reason why this was the area where the fewest African traditions were continued. But there were many other reasons as well. In fact, nearly every aspect of Northeastern life and environment worked against the retention of Africanisms. Climate was one and geography was another. Because of the cold winters and the relatively short growing season, there were no major cash crops and no large plantations needing many slaves. The land was rocky and already overplanted and thus less fertile than the land in other regions. There were many fewer slaves in this area than anywhere else in the New World, and with a ratio of many whites to a few blacks, black slaves here were more intensively exposed to European culture than anywhere else in the New World. Finally, the slaves who were brought to the North American Northeast were rarely brought directly from Africa but rather via the West Indies. As the Northeastern demand for slaves was relatively small, it was not profitable for slavers to bring huge shipments of slaves directly from Africa. If we consider slaves as a commodity and the various areas of the New World as markets, as they were considered by the slavers, then South America, the Caribbean and the North American South can be seen as wholesale markets, buying large quantities of the commodity. The North American Northeast can be seen as a retail market, buying smaller quantities of the commodity from the wholesale markets. Northern shipping firms sent ships regularly to the West Indies taking rum, which was made from molasses and sugar from the West Indies, and bringing back cargoes of molasses and sugar. Slaves became an additional cargo.

Thus, the slaves who arrived in the North American Northeast had already begun to adjust to slavery and to New World culture; in having done so, it was not as difficult to adjust to another area of the New World.

The different degrees of adjustment to various New World areas and the different degrees of contact with whites in these areas had great bearing upon the extent to which the slaves were able to continue their religious, magical and mystical traditions. This will be seen clearly as we look at religions, magical and mystical practices among the slaves and among blacks after the period of slavery.

THE RELIGION OF THE SLAVES

One Africanism that was continued by the slaves in every part of the New World was the pervasiveness of religion and the supernatural.

Not only was this true of the slaves as individuals; it was also true of groups of slaves. Even when religious gatherings were forbidden, their need to worship together was great enough to cause them to take considerable risks to satisfy that need. The following passage tells of secret slave religious ceremonies in Louisiana:

On this plantation there were about one hundred and fifty slaves. Of this number, only about ten were Christians. We can easily account for this, for religious services among the slaves were strictly forbidden. But the slaves would steal away into the woods at night and hold services. They would form a circle on their knees around the speaker who would also be on his knees. He would bend forward and speak into or over a vessel of water to drown the sound. If anyone became animated and cried out, the others would quickly stop the noise by placing their hands over the offender's mouth.[7]

Whether in Paramaribo in Surinam or in Philadelphia, Pennsylvania, the slaves were every minute of their lives conscious of outside forces working upon them and upon others. Partly, of course, this was due to their oppressed condition. As slaves, if they had not believed in powers higher than themselves and higher than their white masters, they could not have survived. Belief in the supernatural gave some meaning to their lives. But the African religious tradition was the major reason; otherwise, other depressed groups would also have turned to religion. The Indians, for example, actually were enslaved in South America; in North America they were so oppressed that they might just as well have been slaves. Yet in both areas the Indians died at an alarming rate, and the reason for such a high death rate cannot be wholly laid upon disease or murder by the whites. A major reason for the high death rate was despair and hopelessness, for the Indians, although they had a highly developed religion based upon Nature, did not have the strong, all-pervasive belief in the supernatural that the black slaves did. They were unable to find a meaning to their lives that was higher than their earthly existence. In the face of the white man's gods, theirs went away.

This was not the case with the black slaves, and this was due not only to the tradition that religion was an inseparable part of daily life. It was also due to the African tradition of accepting new gods.

It will be remembered that one characteristic of African religion was the tendency to accept new gods. Loyalty to a god depended upon his effectiveness and his power. The same sort of pattern occurred among the slaves in the New World, for here they were the conquered and their masters were the conquerors. Obviously the masters' gods must be powerful.

The degree of acceptance of the masters' gods varied in different parts of the New World, specifically between Catholic countries and Protestant countries. In Catholic countries, the slaves were able to accept the gods of their masters without rejecting their own; they were able to combine African religious practices with Catholic practices. In Protestant countries, the slaves were generally forced to choose between their gods and their masters' god, and as time went on they forgot many of their own gods. However, they were able to continue some of their African religious practices under the guise of Christianity.

The Catholic countries were those ruled by the French and the Spanish—Haiti, Santo Domingo, Brazil, French Guiana, Cuba, and, in the United States until 1803, Louisiana. In all these areas it was required by the Church that the slaves be baptized. But this did not cause the slaves to accept Catholicism. What did cause them to adopt certain aspects of Catholicism was the Catholic belief in and worship of saints. The saints were seen by the slaves as minor gods, just like the African minor gods. As time went on, various African spirits who were believed to control certain aspects of nature were each identified with a particular saint. The African spirit cults were revived, only in New World Catholic countries the spirit of each cult was a particular saint, and new members were called either "daughter of the saint" or "son of the saint."

An example of this identification was the Haitian identification of the god Legba (the Dahomean god who watched over entrances and guarded crossroads) with the Catholic St. Peter, guardian of the keys. Almost the same identification was made among slaves in Louisiana, only their god was called Liba, rather than Legba. The Dahomean serpent-deity

Dan, whose color was white, was identified by Haitian slaves with St. Patrick. In Louisiana, Blanc Dani (White Danny) was identified with St. Michael. Some of the reasons for these identifications are obvious, others are not, but there were many, many such identifications of African gods with Catholic saints.

The Protestant countries were those ruled by the English and the Dutch—the British West Indies, British and Dutch Guiana, and, except for Louisiana, the United States. The Protestant religion did not recognize saints, and thus the slaves were faced with the "choice" between their gods and their masters' god. In the United States, as time went on with contact between slaves and whites increasing and whites frowning upon or forbidding African religious practices, the slaves began to worship their masters' god. A further factor, due to the constant contact between slaves and masters, was the increasing identification of the better way of life with the customs of their masters. There was no question that the masters had the power, thus their god must be the most powerful.

In the British West Indies, Trinidad and Tobago, and in British and Dutch Guiana, the situation was different. In these areas where black slaves far outnumbered white slave masters, contact between the two groups was much less close and much less constant. In these areas, depending upon the degree of contact with whites, the slaves' religious practices ran the gamut from purely African rituals to a

Protestantism similar to that of North American slaves, with every degree and gradation in between.

Although in some areas of the New World African gods were retained or blended with new gods and in other areas African gods were lost, in every area the African practice of ancestor worship was continued to some degree.

One of the most general examples of the continuation of ancestor worship among the slaves was the code of respect toward old people. In the North American South it was not the slave masters who began the custom of calling old slaves "Uncle" or "Aunty," but the slaves themselves who from the beginning of slavery referred to old people in this way whether they were relatives or not. Of course respect for one's elders was part of the European code of conduct as well, but there was a definite basis for this conduct among the slaves in African ancestral worship:

. . . it is considered bad luck to . . . "sass" the old folks. This latter idea may have at one time had a real meaning, since the old folks were "almost ghosts," and hence worthy of good treatment lest their spirits avenge the disrespect and actually cause bad luck to the offender.[8]

It will be remembered that in West Africa it was believed that dead ancestors watched over the living members of their family and helped or hurt them, depending upon the respect and honor they received from the living. Among the slaves, there was a belief that, if an escaped slave put graveyard dirt in his shoes, the dogs could not track him. It is probable that this belief is related to ancestor worship. Also in West Africa, a funeral ceremony fitting to honor the dead was extremely important, and this tradition was carried on in the New World:

There was one thing which the Negro greatly insisted upon, and which not even the most hardhearted masters were ever quite willing to deny them. They could never bear that their dead could be put away without a funeral. Not that they expected, at the time of burial, to have the funeral service. Indeed, they did not desire it, and it was never according to their notions. A funeral to them was a pageant. It was a thing to be arranged for a long time ahead. It was to be marked by the gathering of kindred and friends from far and near . . . "The funeral" loomed up weeks in advance, and although marked by sable garments, mournful manners and sorrowful outcries it had about it hints of an elaborate social function with festive accompaniments.[9]

It has been shown that in varying degrees the nature gods and the ancestor gods worshiped in West Africa continued to be worshiped by the slaves in the New World. The "divine trickster" also continued to be worshiped, taking different forms in Catholic and Protestant areas. In all the areas the divine trickster as the youngest child of a particular god did not survive very well, but the divine trickster among the major gods did. As we have already mentioned, in West Africa, he was called Legba or Elegbara, and he watched over entrances and cross-roads. In the Catholic areas of the New World he was carried on, as Legba, Elegbara, Lebba or Liba, and simply identified with St. Peter, the keeper of the keys. In the Protestant areas there was no saint that the trickster could be identified with, but there was another personage that he could be identified with—Satan, or the Devil.

Actually, it was Christian missionaries themselves who began this identification. In Christianity there is complete separation between good and bad; there is no concept that both good and bad could reside in the same thing. Thus, when Protestant missionaries learned of Legba, the divine trickster, who could be good or bad, they naturally decided he was all bad and referred to him as the Devil.

Although in time the slaves in Protestant areas of the New World made this identification themselves, they never equated their god completely with the Devil and never accepted the Protestant concept of the Devil. For the Protestant Devil was all bad, a fallen angel, an avenger who presided over the terrors of hell and held the souls of the damned to their penalties, and the African tradition could never believe in a character who was that bad. Thus, although they called their character the Devil, the slaves did not hate or fear him. They rather liked him, and often laughed at his tricks. In some ways he was a convenience, for all sorts of mishaps could be blamed on him and on his crafty ways. The easy, almost friendly relationship between the slaves and the Devil is revealed in this passage:

The Africans cling to their tendency to worship the malevolent even after they have heard of Christianity. One bishop asked them why they persisted in worshiping the devil instead of God. The reply was, "God is good, God is love and don't hurt anybody—do as you please, God don't hurt you; but do bad and the devil will get you sure! We need not bother about God, but we try to keep on the good side of the devil."[10]

In the persistence among slaves of belief in the divine trickster can also be seen the persistence to look at the world very realistically, not as divided into good and bad but as everywhere both good and bad.

Although it was in the Catholic areas of the New World that the slaves were able to make the greatest number of identifications between their gods and the gods of the slave masters, they were unable to make many identifications between their traditional religious practices and those of the Catholic Church. Catholic rituals were very strictly defined and quite formal, and there was little room for new interpretations by the slaves. By contrast, the Protestant religion, although it did not have saints or beings with which the slaves could identify their many gods, was very flexible in terms of religious practices. There were many branches of the Protestant religion, and their practices ranged from well-defined rituals, similar to those of the Catholic Church, to very informal unrestrained practices. Of these many branches, it was the Baptist Church which attracted the majority of the slaves, and this was because the Baptist Church had many aspects which the slaves could identify with their own religious traditions.

It will be remembered that in West Africa river cults were among the most important religious groups. It was the priests of these river cults who usually were the most stubborn in their refusal to accept the gods of their conquerors and who were most often disposed of by being sold into slavery. It will also be remembered that a major part of worship of river spirits was a pilgrimage to some sacred body of water where the highest form of worship was to be possessed by the river spirit and to fling oneself into the water.

Water was also very important in the Baptist Church, whose name and chief practices both revolved around baptism by water. Although Baptists did not run into the water under possession by God, baptism was supposed to be accompanied by the revelation of God. And in some Baptist churches an experience much like possession did happen to certain worshipers. In addition, it was poor whites who formed the major membership of the Baptist Church, and of all the whites the slaves came into contact with, it was poor whites who seemed least formidable and were least feared. Thus, it was quite natural that the Baptist Church, with its practices of worship involving immersion in a body of water and its humble membership, should receive the greatest influx of slave converts.

One more aspect of the Baptist Church that made it favored among the slaves was its organization, which allowed for great independence in its local churches. Under this organization the slaves, and later the freedmen, could form their own congregations and enjoy great freedom in terms of the way they chose to worship God. As time went on, Negro Baptist congregations became well known for their unique practices. Although their water rituals were those of baptism, as the new member to be baptized was immersed in a stream or a pond and as the spirit descended upon him, often he became possessed and behaved exactly like West African cultists behaved.

Also, among Negro Baptists, the biblical concept of the river Jordan enjoyed increased importance. For them, "crossing the river Jordan" became a symbol of what comes after death. Many Negro spirituals developed with the river Jordan as their theme.

Another African tradition which the slaves were able to introduce into their version of the Baptist religion was the rule that new members go through a period of initiation, called "mourning," before baptism. This was similar to the West African rule that priests go through a period of seclusion while being trained for the priesthood.

Baptist missionaries worked among the slaves in all Protestant areas of the New World, and Negro

Baptist groups could be found everywhere. The greatest similarities between Negro Baptist practices and West African practices were to be found in the West Indies and in South America, due again to less contact with whites as compared to North America. In fact, in an area such as Trinidad, religious practices that were supposedly Baptist came so close to African religious practices that even the flexible leaders of the Baptist Church suspected that they were heresy. This was particularly true of the "spiritual Baptists" of Trinidad.

A spiritual Baptist meeting would begin much like any other Baptist service, with songs from the Sankey and Moody hymnal. But these songs would be sung in a room or building not exactly traditional Baptist. Markings in white chalk on the floor, at the doors and around the center pole were distinctly African. Then a Sankey hymn would be begun and sung over and over, and gradually African rhythms would enter in, the tempo would quicken, and an hour or two after the service had begun it could no longer be called a Baptist service.

There would be no drums and rattles, but the sounds and rhythms of these instruments would be approximated in hand clapping and vocal sounds. Possession would seize first one, then another worshiper. There was no dancing, but those possessed would engage in "patting" the foot. Shoes were removed—in Africa it is part of the etiquette of dancing to do so barefoot. Those possessed would whirl and jump and fall on the floor, shout, and speak in tongues. What had begun as a staid Baptist service had become almost purely African.

Such spiritual or shouting services also occurred among Negro Baptists in the United States and also can be traced quite directly to African survivals. What made them frowned upon less than in Trinidad was that there were a number of white revivalist sects at whose camp meetings similar types of possession and shouting behavior occurred. It is hard to tell how much effect the slaves' practices had upon the white sects, but there was a long tradition of revivalism and religious hysteria in Europe.

So far we have talked about those religious practices among the slaves that were conducted under the guise of Christianity, either Catholic or Protestant, and accepted, although sometimes with strong reservations, by these Christian churches. For the most part, these were the only kinds of religious practices engaged in by the slaves in North America (except in Louisiana) and in the Protestant areas of South America and the Caribbean. The Protestant religion was flexible enough to incorporate a number of Africanisms as long as they were not recognized as Africanisms.

In the Catholic areas, on the other hand, there did not exist that flexibility. Except for the presence of saints with whom the slaves could identify their traditional gods, there was little about Catholicism that the slaves could relate to African religions. Thus, they formed their own cults, incorporating elements of Catholicism with African elements. But these were not recognized by the Catholic Church and were often outlawed.

One such cult was the Brazilian Batuque. The central theme of the Batuque cult was a kind of contract between a human being and a spirit—the human being received the spirit and allowed it to participate in ceremonies, and in return the spirit looked out for the welfare of the human being.

There were hundreds of spirits in the Batuque belief system. The highest were those of the Catholic religion—God, the Virgin Mary, Jesus and the saints and angels. Next there was another class of spirits, chiefly the souls of the dead, who drifted in space between heaven and earth. Even closer to man, living under the earth or in the seas and rivers, were another group of spirits. It was these spirits who were thought to possess people.

These spirits were of various origins and natures. They were even called by various names. Sometimes they were called *vodun* or *orixa*, the Dahomean and Yoruba words for "deity." Sometimes they were called guides, or saints, or invisible ones. Most commonly, they were called *encantados*, or "enchanted ones." It did not bother the members of the Batuque cult that the encantados were not clearly defined or explained; they were considered a mystery, just as God was a mystery.

The Batuque cultists believed that all these supernatural beings, as well as certain inanimate objects such as the sun, moon and stars, had interest, power and influence over the lives of men. The degree of interest, power and influence, however, varied. God, for example, was seen as too far away and too concerned with the problems of the universe to pay much attention to mere human beings. The saints, since they had once lived on earth and since they depended upon man's prayers for their happiness, were more apt to notice man's problems and hear his pleas for help. But even saints were remote and more concerned with questions of the universe. It was the encantados who were closest to human beings and most concerned with their problems. Like people, they could be good and bad; some were given to drinking too much and even the most honored encantados were criticized for their love of dancing and fancy clothes.

Although they were seen as having many of the characteristics of human beings, encantados were also believed to have a wide range of superhuman powers. They could travel on the wind, hear humans calling them no matter where they were, keep watch over humans from any distance and, very importantly, predict the future.

The encantados were believed to be able to cause strangers to behave in ways that would help their worshipers. They could cause employers to offer jobs, wealthy people to make contributions to the cults, an admired person to fall in love with his admirer.

However, the encantados also had the power to cause calamities and accidents, sometimes as punishment for the human beings involved and sometimes simply to remind humans of their power.

Encantados could also descend and take possession of a person's body. It was believed that the person's own spirit was forced outside his body by the encantado and remained nearby ready to re-enter when the encantado left. Some encantados were thought to be able to perform feats that would cause damage to the body of an unpossessed person. They might walk on live coals or wash their hands in boiling oil or burn gunpowder in the palm of their hand.

Encantados were believed to be everywhere, to own everything in nature as well as certain man-made things. For example, an empty house was believed to be immediately claimed by the encantados who owned the land on which the house stood. As long as they were properly worshiped and honored, the encantados could bring luck and success. If they were somehow insulted, they could steal and hide human possessions, open and slam doors or windows, rap loudly on walls, or appear as animal or human ghosts that melted away as one approached them. Like the religion of their forefathers in Africa, the religion of the slaves in Brazil was very much a part of everyday life.

Although the individual's relationship with encantados was much like his relationship with Catholic saints—the person promised to do something that would please the encantado if the encantado would grant his or her request—individuals more often did not deal directly with the encantados. Usually, they communicated with the encantados through a medium. Mediums were thought to have a very special close relationship with the encantados, especially with one particular encantado. They called this particular encantado their father or mother and called themselves son or daughter. The medium was thus the earthly child of the spirit, and the spirit was believed to watch over his "child" as a good parent would. The medium did not choose his special encantado, the spirit chose him. The spirit seized or possessed the medium, and in this way began their special relationship. Once this special relationship became known, believers would visit the medium. If the medium was under the possession of the spirit at the time, the believer approached the encantado through the medium, asking that a particular request be granted and asking what special acts he could perform in return to please the encantado. Then, through the medium, the encantado would order that herb baths be taken or that candles be lit or that some contribution be made to the medium. The believer would do as he was bid and then wait for his request to be granted. If it was not granted, he would simply visit a medium who was possessed by another encantado. As in Africa, there was no rule of absolute loyalty to a particular god.

Needless to say, Church authorities disapproved of this worship of encantados. Worship of saints was one thing; worship of supernatural beings who could be bad or good, who could drink too much or who could be too vain about their clothing, was quite another. In the eyes of the Church, worship of encantados was not really religion at all.

This was often true of slave cults in the New World, but the inability to draw a line between religion and other supernatural or magical practices was not a new problem. It will be remembered that the distinction between witchcraft and religion in West Africa was very fuzzy. The same was true of these New World cults, among them the Batuque. But the foremost New World cult that crossed the line between religion and magic was the *vodun* cult. Was it chiefly a religious or a magical system? It is hard to say. Like the Batuque cult, it will be treated between the section on the religious practices of the slaves and that of the magical practices of the slaves. The vodun cult, though, definitely leans more toward the magical than the religious, although it contains elements of both.

Like the Batuque cult, the cult of vodun began in the Catholic areas of the New World. The word *vodun* comes from the West African Ewe tribe and is derived from *vo* (apart), which can be interpreted to mean "set apart" or "holy." Vodun was a serpent cult in West Africa and although different tribes worshiped serpent-deities of different names, these serpent cults were very much alike in practices and beliefs. In the New World, vodun enjoyed its first and most lasting prominence in Haiti and Santo Domingo, where the serpent-god Damballa, the Dahomean serpent-god Dan, was worshiped. In nearly all of these cults, the priestess was more important than the priest. It was the priestess who danced around the fires to the beat of the drums, who danced around the bubbling caldron of liquid in the center of the gathering. It was the priestess who lifted the cult's snake from his box—traditionally, it was a python—and allowed it to lick her cheek. From this touch she received vision and power and became a foreteller of the future. Then, other believers could ask her questions about their futures or make requests of the serpent-god. As we know this system as voodoo rather than as vudun, the term voodoo will be used here.

Like the Brazilian Batuque, the voodoo practiced by the slaves in Haiti and Santo Domingo was a mixture of African and Catholic religious elements. Basically, it was the worship of an all-powerful and supernatural being symbolized by a serpent and of a host of lesser *loa* who surrounded him. Eventually, these loa were identified with the saints of the Catholic Church, although their African names were kept. For instance, one of these lesser gods was Ogu-Badagri (Badagri is a town in Nigeria), and another was Ezili-Freda-Dahomey (Ezili of Whydah-Dahomey). It was a strong system, and by the 1790's voodoo was, in Haiti and Santo Domingo, very close to being an organized church, with temples, *bokono* (magicians) and *vodu-no* (priests) who had been trained in Africa, elaborate ritual and ceremonial dancing.

Voodoo was a religion in that the all-powerful serpent-god was a god of goodness—a god "too good to get angry." Like Christianity, it was a religion of the people, explaining for them the nature of the world in which they lived, the terrifying experiences of their captivity in a strange land, and the ways they could, under the skilled guidance of medicine men and priests, protect themselves from the ever-present evil. They sought deliverance from evil that was seen and unseen through faithfulness to the great serpent-god and reverence of the lesser loa. Elaborate rituals were performed in worship of these gods in which live snakes were used and in which the priests and priestesses were possessed by the serpent-spirits.

From the beginning, however, like African religions, voodoo was also a magical system. Charms to ward off evil were an important part of any believer's possessions. And the conditions of slavery were such that charms to work evil soon became important as well. Under these conditions, the African slaves were soon in conflict with one another and with the slave masters over color, status and the brutality of forced labor. This situation arose everywhere in the New World where slavery was practiced, but it arose particularly in the Caribbean and in South America. The fact that there was little contact between whites and slaves in these areas and thus little opportunity for these groups to know and understand each other meant that there was greater hostility and tension between them. Also, the large ratio of slaves to owners gave the slaves a certain sense of power, as did the greater opportunities for escape presented by forested, mountainous and little populated terrain. The fear and hatred which magic and witchcraft often represented came to be a part of a religion that tried to deal with the horrors of slavery.

In Haiti, voodoo became an inseparable part of the militant yearning for freedom of the slaves. The "maroons," or fugitive slaves, who held out in the mountains and spurred a slave rebellion in 1758 had their priests with them and faithfully practiced voodoo rites. One of these maroons was a voodoo prophet or magician named Makandal. He predicted the future, he had visions and he was an extremely powerful speaker. He caused the other slaves to believe he was immortal, and he managed to put them in such terror and respect that they felt it an honor to serve him and to worship him as they would a god. Escaping from his master's plantation, Makandal spread terror by pillaging plantations, sacking villages, stealing cattle and poisoning both blacks and whites. He was later burned at the stake at Limbé in northern Haiti, but legends about his escape from the fire continued for years. Later, his name was often called by those who wished to inspire antiwhite resistance.

Jean François was another early Haitian rebel who used voodoo to his advantage. He surrounded himself with sorcerers and filled his tent with cats of all colors, dead men's bones and other symbolic objects. At night, wild dances were held in his camp of escaped slaves, and when the excitement had reached its peak, his lieutenant, Biassou, would appear before the crowd, followed by his magicians. Biassou would cry that the spirit of God was inspiring him and that he had been instructed to announce that all fighters who died in battle would return again to their tribes in Africa. Great exaltation would follow Biassou's appearance, and he and Jean François would seize upon the time to lead their men against the enemy in the middle of the night.

In 1791 the slaves in Haiti and Santo Domingo revolted successfully, and in doing so they invoked all the powers of voodoo. The man who is credited with starting the revolt was a Jamaican-born slave named Boukman. In the summer of 1791 he escaped from the Haitian plantation to which he had been sold, taking with him a number of other slaves. In the weeks that followed, his army grew, but they were not united, as they had to be in order to conduct a successful revolt. To bring about the needed unity, Boukman conducted an impressive ceremony on the night of August 14. After a large crowd had gathered, a violent storm arose, and in the midst of thunder and lightning an old black woman appeared, danced wildly, sang and flashed a huge cutlass over her head. Finally, the silent and fascinated crowd saw her plunge the cutlass into the throat of a black hog. The slaves drank the animal's blood and swore they would follow Boukman's orders. Six days later Boukman led his rebels in a mass slaughter of whites the likes of which the island had never known before. A general slave revolt followed, and eventually all of Haiti was controlled by the slaves.

Toussaint L'Ouverture emerged as the leader of

the revolution and as the first black leader of Haiti. He had been a medicine man, or "root doctor," and had often sought divination, or the foretelling of the future, from voodoo priests. Although he was a staunch Roman Catholic, he and other leaders of the revolution insisted that it was the mystical powers of the voodoo priests that gave the black fighters their strength and drove the English, Spanish, and finally the army of Napoleon into the sea. L'Ouverture's successor, Jean Jacques Dessalines, had been a plantation slave, and it is said that he knew voodoo better than his predecessor. Yet both L'Ouverture and Dessalines launched strong anti-voodoo campaigns after they came to power, obviously fearing that their enemies might successfully use voodoo against them. But voodoo continued in Haiti, and despite their antivoodoo stands, both L'Ouverture and Dessalines joined Makandal as Haitian voodoo saints. Revealing of how important the magical aspects of voodoo became in Haiti is the fact that after the revolution, the *P'tit Albert*, a book of medieval European magic, was so feared that its importation into the country was prohibited by law.

Meanwhile, voodoo had been known in North America as well, carried by slaves imported directly from Africa as well as by the many slaves who came to the mainland by way of the West Indies. Elements of voodoo were reported in parts of Georgia and South Carolina. In Louisiana, which had been settled first by the French and then by the Spanish, in 1782 the Spanish Governor Gálvez issued an order banning the importation of all blacks from the French West Indian island of Martinique because he believed them to be steeped in voodooism.

Laws such as this kept the practice of voodoo to a minimum in North America. Other laws against slaves assembling together also kept voodoo down. Plantations were widely separated, and the slaves of various estates did not often meet. Old slaves passed on a few of the superstitions, remembered a few of the charms known to their African ancestors, but for the most part voodoo was being forgotten. Then, beginning in 1791 and lasting for some thirteen years after, an influx of refugees brought voodoo full blown to North America, especially to Louisiana.

The refugees were French planters, their slaves and black freedmen who had escaped from the slave revolution in Haiti and Santo Domingo. Some had sought shelter on neighboring islands—Trinidad, Jamaica, Guadeloupe, Puerto Rico. Most had found a haven on Santiago de Cuba, across the Windward Passage from Santo Domingo, but when, in 1809, France invaded Spain, they were forced by Spanish Cuba to leave. Some ten thousand of these once-again refugees found their way to New Orleans, swelling both the white and black populations.

The blacks from Haiti and Santo Domingo arrived in Louisiana steeped in the knowledge and practice of voodoo. For the most part they settled in New Orleans. Those who were slaves settled in or near the city because their masters found it to their liking.

Those who were freedmen settled in the city because urban centers offered the greatest opportunities for free blacks. Once settled, black refugees sought each other out to rekindle the flame of voodooism. New Orleans blacks, who remembered or who had heard of voodoo, were eager to join the refugees in their rites.

It is said that the first gathering place of the voodoos in New Orleans was an abandoned brick-yard, where they met late at night for their dances and rituals. Then, when the police drove them from that place, they began to hold their meetings along the shore of Lake Pontchartrain.

There were many versions of these ceremonies. It will be remembered that in the African rites the priestess allowed the snake to lick her cheek and thus received vision and power. In Louisiana, the priestess was more often called a queen. Sometimes she stood upon the box which housed the snake and passed the power to the king and the others by simply beginning a chain of handclasping. At other times the king lifted the box and shook it, and from the numerous bells which always decorated it came a magic tinkling that hypnotized the worshipers and caused them to become closer to the god.

Sometimes the serpent-god, who in Louisiana was usually called the Zombi, was represented by a male dancer. A great caldron would be set to boiling over a fire in the center of the clearing in which the ceremonies were being held, and into it would be tossed offerings brought by the worshipers—chickens, frogs, cats, snails and always a snake. The queen would begin to chant: "He is coming, the Great Zombi, he is coming, to make *gris-gris* [charms]!" The male dancer would leap into the center of the clearing and begin a whirling dance, whirling and whirling until he collapsed from sheer exhaustion. Then the others would dance, stopping periodically to drink the contents of the caldron. They would dance and drink and dance and drink until they too were possessed. They had the power.

Sacrifice and the drinking of blood were always a part of these early voodoo rituals. Usually the blood of a young lamb was used, but often it was that of a black cat. Another important part was the eating of raw flesh. In the frenzy of possession the worshipers would tear animals, usually chickens, apart with their bare hands and eat them raw.

It was required that a new member of the cult be initiated and that he become possessed before the actual cult rituals began. The king would draw a circle on the ground with a piece of charcoal, and the new member was ordered to stand in the circle. Certain charms were given him—a wax figure of a man, a bit of human bone and some horsehairs. The king would then strike him on the head with a wooden paddle and begin a chant in an African dialect. Other cult members, who were standing around the circle, would repeat each word in chorus. At last the initiate would begin to tremble and jerk, for he would have begun to get the power. As the power increased within him, his movements would become wilder and wilder. But he had to be careful and not step outside the circle. If he did, the voodoos would turn their backs on him, for they considered this an evil omen. Carefully remaining within the circle, the initiate would dance faster and faster until he fell down in a dead faint. The king would then rouse him with a sharp blow of the wooden paddle, give him the oath of the voodoos and the initiate would then become a member of the cult.

Although so far we have spoken several times of voodoo kings, actually they were minor figures in the cults. Voodoo was, from the beginning, female-oriented. The only men of importance were the witch doctors. The voodoo queens were the important cult leaders. Nearly all the voodoo songs were about the queens. Women, too, seemed to comprise the majority of the cultists, at least eighty per cent, and not all of these were black women.

Almost from the beginning of the organized practice of voodoo in New Orleans, white women could be found among the cultists. Usually they joined because they sought the power to gain or to regain the affection of a man they loved. Sometimes white men joined in the ceremonies, but they usually were not true believers and were just looking for attractive women.

The fact that whites did join these cults or at least attended their ceremonies bothered the authorities, but it was not for this reason that the authorities began to issue ordinances designed to destroy the voodoo cults. In 1803, New Orleans had become an American Territory through the Louisiana Purchase. By 1813 the idea of racial uprising again became important and officials began to suspect and fear that the voodoos were involved. It was known that voodoos were stirring up hatred against their white masters and that some of their meetings were held for the purpose of working black magic against the whites, if not to plot actual revolution. Some voodoo sympathizers called this fear on the part of the authorities groundless, but there is evidence that they had good reason for fear. In the first place, voodoo by its nature was a rebellious cult. In the second place, it was fact that the revolting slaves in Haiti and Santo Domingo had openly used voodoo to inspire their followers. In the third place, the voodoos had added a new saint to their pantheon, or group of beings they worshiped. This was St. Marron (or Maron). Runaway slaves were traditionally called "maroons," or "marons" in French-speaking areas. St. Marron was worshiped as the patron saint of runaway slaves, and obviously the voodoos would not have had such a saint if they did not support whatever means of gaining freedom were available to the slaves. In 1817 an ordinance was passed forbidding slaves to dance anywhere or at any time except in Congo Square in New Orleans on Sunday. The slaves did indeed take to dancing in Congo Square on Sundays, and their dances were famous for over twenty years. However, they continued their illegal voodoo ceremonies out by Lake Pontchartrain.

There, it was more and more often whispered, they offered human sacrifices. Although there is little proof that such sacrifices were made, on occasion voodoos were heard referring to the "goat without horns," an expression common in Haiti and meaning the sacrifice of a young white child. The queens were always being accused of kidnaping and murdering children, and for many years New Orleanians believed that every small child that disappeared had become a voodoo sacrifice.

Antivoodoo activities and statements by city officials were strongest about 1820 and again in the late 1830's. In the late 1830's the slaves were forbidden even to dance in Congo Square on Sundays, again because of fears of a slave uprising. Although this ordinance was repealed in the 1840's, antivoodooism continued and increased to such an extent that by 1850 the New Orleans newspapers were defending the voodoos. Perhaps it was the knowledge that the newspapers were on their side that caused the voodoo women to begin publicly defending themselves against police accusations. When arrested on charges of working black magic or holding indecent ceremonies, they refused to admit the charges and argued that their voodoo practices were purely religious. The newspapers gave extensive coverage to these incidents, and a number of voodoo queens gained considerable fame through them. The most famous was Marie Laveau, about whom more will be told in a later chapter. Meanwhile, the kings and other male practitioners of voodoo went about their daily business, but it is probable that they, too, profited from the newspaper coverage of voodooism by getting more customers.

The majority of the time of both male and female voodoo leaders was spent not in presiding over ceremonies and dances but in dispensing advice and charms to people who visited them in need of help. The charms, called gris-gris, came in many forms. One voodoo priestess specialized in making and selling gris-gris bags containing charms and bottles containing direct curses. The most important male voodoo leader of the first half of the nineteenth century, Dr. John, specialized not only in the selling of gris-gris but also in healing and in the telling of fortunes. He placed and lifted curses for a fee. He sold tiny bottles containing love potions to women of every age and color. Men paid large sums of money for a shell wrapped in a twist of human hair or a packet of talcum powder which they believed would help them win the affection of the women they loved. Dr. Jack, who operated in New Orleans during the same period as Dr. John, was especially noted for his love charms—beef hearts, perfumed and decorated with toads' feet, spider claws and satin ribbons like valentines. Female voodoo leader Marie Saloppé is said to have made a small fortune from the sale of brick dust at a nickel a bucket. An African and a voodoo tradition was that washing the front steps of one's house with a special solution would wash away an evil omen placed on the house by an enemy. In New Orleans, brick dust came to be the special solution, and many stoops had a well-scrubbed, whitish appearance, showing that brick-dust had been used.

It is in these practices of using charms and curses, of healing and foretelling the future that voodoo becomes a magical system rather than a religious system. In fact, sometimes all magic and witchcraft among New World blacks are referred to as voodoo, or "hoodoo," a North American Negro version of voodoo. As in Africa, there was no distinct line that could be drawn between the black slaves' religion and their witchcraft and magic.

THE MAGIC OF THE SLAVES

African magical traditions were to survive among the slaves in the New World even better than their religious traditions. Partly this was due to the fact that witchcraft and magic could be more effectively practiced by individuals and did not depend upon ceremonies or dancing or other rituals that required the participation of a group of people. Although the white masters could forbid the slaves from meeting or congregating in groups and could keep a close watch on the slave quarters to see that their orders were obeyed, it was impossible for them to prevent an individual slave from making up a bag of nail parings and strands of hair or from mixing some sort of potion, or from placing a silent curse upon another. Magic also remained very alive and vital among the slaves because it was especially adaptable to the conditions of slavery. Magic accepts the general conditions of one's life and does not attempt to change one's status. It simply helps the individual to feel protected from his neighbor or to hurt his neighbor, to win the affection of one he loves or to make small gains. Its main value is psychological. In the early years of slavery there were many slave revolts and other attempts by the slaves to gain their freedom. But as time went on and the slaves realized that freedom was far beyond their reach, making their lives under slavery as bearable as possible became their chief goal, and for this magic was very important.

Another reason for the survival of African magical practices among the slaves was the lack of any threat from European magical practices and beliefs. While Protestant and Catholic missionaries worked hard at converting the slaves to their religions; no white magician tried to convert the slaves to belief in his magic. Even so, especially in the United States, a number of Negro beliefs and practices can be said to be derived from European origins. This is true in the United States because of the historically closer contact between the slaves and their masters. A slave working in the master's house might overhear some European folk belief or superstition and adopt it, eventually spreading it among the other slaves on the plantation. Of course this influencing could and did work both ways. The whites would overhear a slave superstition and adopt it. In the West Indies and in South America, where there was less contact between whites and slaves, there was less chance of this mutual influencing, although it occurred even in those areas.

In some cases, African and European magical beliefs and practices simply were similar to one another without mutual influencing. Although the purpose of this book is to point out the differences between the white world and the black world in the area of witchcraft, mysticism and magic, the truth that men, no matter what their origin or color, are basically alike should not be forgotten. Compare all the major world religions and you will find that there are more similarities than differences. All men must believe in a power or powers higher than themselves that rule the universe. All men must also believe that something orders and controls their relationship with others. Compare magical practices and folk beliefs all around the world and again you will find more similarities than differences.

For instance, West Africans believed that if you buried a bag of hair clippings and nail parings under a man's doorstep he would die. Europeans believed in the same procedure, except that the man would only become ill. West Africans believed that sleeping in the moonlight caused paralysis of one side of the face. Europeans believed sleeping in the moonlight would cause insanity. West Africans believed that if a man went to bed hungry he would lie awake and thus give an unfriendly spirit a chance to take away his soul. Europeans believed that going to bed hungry would merely cause a man to sin. Although these three examples of folk beliefs reveal differences between West Africa and Europe, they also show great similarities. Thus, although it is probable that the slaves were influenced by some of their masters' beliefs and practices, basically their beliefs and practices came directly from their homeland.

As in West Africa, the slaves in the New World made a strong distinction between medical practitioners and conjurers, between those who practiced good magic and those who practiced bad magic. Medical practitioners dealt in herbs, roots, barks and tea, made healing potions and remedies and gave advice to those who sought good things, such as health or happiness in love. Unlike West Africa, with its medicine men, medical practitioners among the slaves at least in the United States were predominantly women. In West Africa medical practitioners and magicians dressed differently but could belong to either sex; this was also true in the West Indies.

Although those who practiced medicine claimed to have supernatural power, true knowledge of the properties of roots and herbs and barks was equally important. Some received this knowledge suddenly like a thunderbolt from the sky and claimed to have been "possessed" with the power. Some learned their craft through apprenticeship to an older practitioner, who may or may not have been a relative. Some simply desired to learn about herbs, learned, had a few opportunities to use what they had learned and continued to gain knowledge and experience until they had earned a reputation. Occasionally, they claimed that during a crisis they received help from a voice that told them the proper remedies.

Conjurers or magicians also had healing powers, but they were more likely to use their power for evil purposes. Supernatural support was all-important for them, much more important than for medical practitioners. Unlike those who practiced medicine, conjurers were very secretive about the source of their power, and a man could not become a conjurer simply through study or simply because he wanted to. Usually, conjuring was an inherited craft. The son was expected to follow in the footsteps of his father; if he did not he would be punished by bad luck or sickness. A man who was not the son of a conjurer could be selected for training by older magicians, but only if he was a "seven month" child or if he was born with a veil over his face. These provisions had to do with the fact that conjurers were much more dependent upon the spirits of dead ancestors than upon God.

In Dutch Guiana in South America conjurers were believed to rely more heavily on the supernatural than medicine men, while in Haiti the fact that the medicine man's art was called a treatment and the magician's art was called a conjure reveals the same distinction. Of course the importance in West Africa of revelation in giving remedies has already been mentioned—it will be remembered that the forest spirits in Dahomey sometimes gave persons information that made them healers.

As in West Africa, conjuration among New World

slaves operated as much as possible on the principle of "like to like." If harm was sought for an enemy, you could have a much more powerful conjure if you were able to obtain something that belonged to your enemy than if you were not. Hair clippings and nail parings were carefully watched lest they fall into strange hands and be used against their owner.

Names were also important in conjures. It will be remembered that in West Africa a child was given a "real" name at birth and that it was kept secret lest a witch learn it and use it against him. In the United States, a slave child was given a "basket name," which was used only by family and close friends.

As in West Africa, the belief that a frizzled hen kept in the yard would scratch up and destroy all conjures was carried over in the West Indies and the North American South.

Although in the New World the West African witch seems to have been replaced by the conjurer, the slaves did believe in witches. Usually, they were believed to be old women and, like the West African witches, to shed their skins and "ride" people in their sleep. As in West Africa, the slaves believed a witch could be destroyed if she were prevented from climbing back into her skin. Salt and pepper sprinkled in the skin was the most common method. One could also sprinkle mustard seed in front of her door while she was out and she would be prevented from getting back in.

The West African belief in "little people" was

also carried over among the slaves to a certain extent. For instance, although food and drink were not actually placed on the floor for the little people, in Haiti, Trinidad and Guiana what fell to the ground during the meal was not swept up the same day since the spirits had caused these morsels to fall in order to eat them. In Dutch Guiana the slaves believed in small dwarfs called *bakru*. Half wood and half flesh, these bakru were "given" by a practitioner of evil magic to a client who wished wealth. If someone tried to strike them they would turn their wooden side to him and then kill him.

Similar to this belief was the idea among slaves in the United States of the tar baby. But unlike the bakru, who were dwarfs, the tar baby was huge, and in this respect is perhaps closer to the West African forest monsters. A man who grew up in southern Georgia during the period of slavery recalls the belief in the tar baby:

As I heard it in one of the southernmost counties of the State, the tar-baby was by no means a mere manufactured, lifeless snare, but a living creature whose body, through some mysterious freak of nature, was composed of tar, and whose black lips were ever parted in an ugly grin. This monster tar-baby, which haunted the woods and lonely places about the plantation, was represented as wholly vicious in character, ever bent upon ensnaring little folks into its yielding, though vice-like embrace. Well do I remember the dread of encountering the ogre-like creature in some remote spot, where I should be unable to withstand its fascinations; for it was said to be impossible to pass the tar-baby without striking it, so provoking was its grin and so insulting its behavior generally, —and when once you had struck it, you were lost. I was always on the lookout for it, but, it is needless to say, I never encountered it, except in dreamland, where again and again was suffered the unspeakable horror of being caught and held stuck fast in its tarry embrace.[11]

Superstitions and minor rituals abounded among Africans in the New World just as they did in Africa. Only a few will be given here, because, first, not much research has been done on the superstitions of the slaves, and, second, most superstitions held by blacks after slavery were the same or similar to those held by blacks during slavery. The superstitions of freed blacks and of blacks today will be treated extensively in the next chapter.

As in West Africa, many superstitions and rituals centered around infants and young children. The idea that a young child did not have a very good "hold" upon his soul was continued among slaves in Mississippi, where it was believed a child would die if he were named before he was a month old. It was as if the spirit were being given a chance to "get used" to the surroundings before it was pegged down. When the baby was a month old he was carried all around the house and brought back into the house through the front door. His spirit having been shown all about, the child was at last named.

In South Carolina, the practice of "calling" the soul of a child before going on a journey was continued.

Names retained their importance. It has already been noted that West African "real" names were similar to U.S. slaves' "basket" names. Also as in West Africa a slave could have a number of different names, which caused great confusion among whites.

As slaves, blacks in the New World had to work whenever their masters wanted them to, and had to do whatever their masters wanted them to do. But it was reported that slaves in parts of South Carolina were very reluctant to work on what they called Green Thursday, for they believed God would send fire down from the heavens and kill them. The parallel with the West African fear of the wrath of the thunder gods is clear. In many parts of the New World, slaves were also reluctant to burn the wood of a tree struck by lightning, for they believed the tree was the property of the thunder gods.

That the slaves brought to the New World carried with them their traditions, and that they retained many of those traditions, especially in the areas of mysticism, witchcraft and magic, throughout slavery is clear. What is hard to understand is why so much of this heritage was retained. After all, the test of all faith, all beliefs and all practices is that they work, and how can the slaves' belief in and practice of mysticism, witchcraft and magic have *worked* if they did not enable them to escape slavery? How could they have *worked* if the whites had been unaffected by them? The answer goes back to the West African sense of reality stressed in this chapter and the last. Supernatural and magical powers could be effective only where there was belief. Where there was no belief there was no power. Supernatural and magical practices worked among blacks because they believed and had been taught these practices from childhood. Many of these practices were completely strange to the whites, and they probably could not have believed even if they had wanted to. The slaves, with their traditional sense of reality, simply accepted the fact that white man's magic wasn't black man's magic.

Chapter 4

Witchcraft, Mysticism and Magic in the Black World Today

There is no slavery in the New World now. Emancipation occurred at different times and for different reasons in various areas. Although these differences were important in terms of the retention of Africanisms, they did not change the order of the list given in the last chapter. Dutch Guiana and Haiti were high on the list, and although the Haitian slaves emancipated and have governed themselves for well over a hundred years, while the slaves of Dutch

Guiana, now called Surinam, were emancipated by their masters and are still governed by the Dutch, both remain in their respective places on the list.

What has changed are the number and degree of Africanisms that have been retained throughout the New World as a whole. In every area there are fewer Africanisms than there were in the time of slavery. This is natural. Over three hundred years have passed since the first slave ship arrived in the New World; some one hundred and fifty years have passed since the slaves successfully revolted in Haiti and Santo Domingo; over one hundred years have passed since the emancipation of the slaves in the United States. Only the very oldest blacks can remember slavery. The slaves who had been born in Africa passed the African traditions on to their children, who passed them on to their children, who in turn passed them on to their children. If you think of a generation as being twenty years, then there have been fifteen generations since the beginning of slavery. That is a long time to keep alive the traditions of another land.

This is not to say that no slaves were brought to the New World during those fifteen generations. Large numbers of blacks from Africa were legally received in the United States between 1800 and 1810; after 1810, they came in as contraband until the outbreak of the Civil War. These slaves, bringing as they did fresh traditions from Africa, probably helped those slaves who had been in the United States for some time and who had received knowledge of African traditions second- or third- or fourth-hand to "remember" some of the traditions in pure form. Undoubtedly, these late-arriving slaves helped the continuation of Africanisms. Even so, more than a century has passed since the last slave arrived from Africa, and it is much more likely that he learned the ways of the older slaves than that they learned his ways. At any rate, if slavery had not lasted as long as it did, and if, in many areas, blacks had not been treated as second-class citizens after emancipation, not nearly as many Africanisms as survive today would have survived. Until fairly recently, for example, few Americans outside of scholarly circles even realized that certain black American activities and customs and types of behavior are influenced by African traditions. Now we are beginning to understand that they are.

The most noticeable aspect of black life throughout the New World is the great importance of the supernatural. Whether it be in the superstitions of blacks in New Orleans or in the worship of encantados in Brazil or in the vitality of the black Baptist churches in the United States, the supernatural is ever present in black daily life. During slavery, its presence could be explained in part by the conditions of slavery. After emancipation, its presence among blacks in areas where they were treated as second-class citizens could be explained by the conditions of second-class citizenship. At all times it can also be explained in terms of the African tradition that the supernatural is an inseparable part of daily life.

RELIGION IN THE BLACK WORLD

Perhaps the second most noticeable aspect of black life throughout the New World is its concern with death, particularly with funerals, and its respect for elderly people. In Protestant countries, this can be explained in part by black religion. Black militants in the United States, for example, criticize their people for concentrating on life after death, on getting their "pie in the sky" after they die instead of directing their energies toward obtaining their rights and enjoying "the good life" right here on earth. It is true that the black Baptist churches greatly stress life after death, but blacks in Catholic countries also show a great concern with death and old people. At least some of this concern is due to the African tradition, however little-remembered, of ancestor worship.

Among New World blacks the funeral, the ceremonial to the dead, remains very important. In the United States, ever since emancipation, blacks have formed mutual-aid societies whose chief purpose has been to ensure proper burial for their members. Even now, among Southern blacks, burial insurance is considered more important than health or accident insurance. It is no accident that one of the most successful occupations in the black community is that of an undertaker.

As in Africa and as among the slaves, a funeral is an important event and one which relatives and friends from far and near should attend. Therefore, it is still not uncommon to have a funeral several weeks after death, in order that it be a proper funeral. The wake is also very important both in the West Indies and the United States, as it is in Africa. The importance of funerals and wakes can also be found among other underprivileged classes of European heritage, but there are certain aspects of black funerals that are not found among those of European ancestry.

For one thing, those who speak at funerals of persons of European ancestry speak only of the good characteristics of the deceased. To speak ill of him would be considered lack of respect. At black funerals, however, both the good and bad characteristics of the dead person are mentioned. Partly, this is due to blacks' and Africans' sense of reality—goodness and badness can be found in everything and in everyone. But it can also be said to be due to the original belief, which now may not even be remembered, that the spirit of the person is listening and if differences he had with those still listening are not mentioned they will be remembered by the spirit and cause his supernatural existence to be troubled to the extent that he will return to trouble the living.

Those of European heritage are not unduly troubled if someone without relatives or burial insurance is simply buried unceremoniously by town officials. Blacks are. An extremely poor man without relatives or burial insurance died in the village of Toco, Trinidad, in 1939. As there was no one to arrange for his burial, village authorities took charge of it. They had a coffin made, dug a grave in the cemetery, and buried him, without ceremony, without even the presence of a minister. All the nonwhite people of the town expressed deep concern that the man had not had any sort of ceremony or funeral. No one was surprised when, a few days later, some children on their way home from school passed the man's hut and saw "him" glaring at them from the branches of a nearby tree. Although the door of his hut was blown open by the wind, no one tried to shut it, for they believed the hut to be haunted by an angry and dissatisfied spirit.

Although those of European heritage often wear black and decorate the house of a dead person with black crepe, some blacks in the American South, for example, tie black crepe on every living thing that comes into the house after the body has been taken out—even on dogs and chickens.

There are certain things that those of European ancestry do that can be called "formal leave-taking" of the dead, such as placing flowers on the coffin or shoveling a spadeful of dirt into the grave. There are more and different formal leave-takings by blacks. The custom of passing young children over the coffin, found in West Africa, has been reported in Surinam, or Dutch Guiana, and in the Sea Islands of South Carolina. In the Sea Islands, this is most often done when a mother dies, for it is believed that her spirit will haunt the baby and worry him in his sleep.

Also in the South Carolina Sea Islands the fruit trees in an orchard are sometimes notified of the death of their owner, for it is believed they, too, will die if they are not told.

Other beliefs and practices surrounding death among New World blacks have been traced to West Africa. It is thought to be bad for anyone to work around a dead person until he is tired, for in such a weakened condition the dead person's spirit might be able to take the tired person's soul. Among bush blacks in Surinam, digging a grave takes several days, for a worker must not allow a single drop of perspiration to fall into the grave. The ghost would use this to take with him the soul of the one who had worked too hard. The spirits of dead people who died in a strange or terrible manner were considered dangerous, and various means were employed to make sure their bodies remained quiet, such as fastening their feet together or weighting them down. Even those who died contented were believed to return at times to places they knew when alive, and at those times feasts had to be provided for them.

Other beliefs among New World blacks, especially in the U. S. South and in the Bahamas, have not been documented as West African retentions, but that is not to say that they will not be in the future. Church members, for example, are buried with their feet to the east so that they will arise on the "last day" facing the rising sun. Sinners are buried facing the opposite direction, as it is believed that they will wish to hide their faces from God.

A spirit newly released from a body tends to be destructive. Thus if there is a clock in the death room, a cloth is put over its face, and if there is a mirror it, too, is covered. Otherwise, the clock will never run again and the mirror will cast no more reflections.

When it rains at a funeral, it is believed that the dead person so displeased God that He wishes to wash the tracks of the dead person from the earth.

It is believed that it is not good to answer the first time your name is called, for it may be a spirit calling you and if you answer the call you will die shortly. Spirits never call more than once at a time, so if your name is called a second time you can answer without fear.

In general, old people are respected more among New World blacks than among New World whites. In the United States, old black people are rarely found homeless, wandering along city streets; old white people often are. Old black people are rarely found in nursing homes; old white people are. Partly, this is a class question—underprivileged classes are more likely to have aunts, grandparents, cousins included in a family unit living under one roof. Partly, this is a financial question—most blacks cannot afford the high prices charged by nursing homes for the care of old people. But partly also, reverence among blacks for their old people is a long tradition, reaching back to the African belief that old people are "almost dead" and thus should be treated with a reverence similar to the reverence of dead ancestors who watch over and either help or hurt their living relatives.

In Haiti, in Guiana, in Trinidad, and in Jamaica it is the right of any elder to whip a younger person for wrongdoing. Usually, it is children who are whipped, but in Haiti, on occasion, a grown man will kneel before his father or uncle to receive a punishment by whipping.

Ancestors continue to be worshiped in Brazil by the Batuque, but as in slavery times they are still believed to be a little too remote from earth to be concerned with man's everyday problems.

In terms of other African gods, most are not worshiped or even remembered by blacks in the New World except in those Catholic countries where they were identified with saints and the tradition was allowed to continue. In the Protestant countries, however, one god who was allowed to continue during slavery continues still today. It will be remembered that the African divine trickster, because he embodied both good and bad, was immediately identified by Christian missionaries as the Devil. The slaves thus were allowed to make the same identification, and the divine trickster remained alive. The Devil is still very much alive among blacks, and he is considered in much the same way as he was considered by West Africans and by the slaves—as a terror but at the same time as a source of enjoyment. Black comedian Flip Wilson used to do a routine in which a woman was always getting into trouble with her husband because she could not resist buying new hats and new dresses. Every time he asked why she bought something, she screamed, "The Devil made me do it!" The Devil, as he always was, is a convenient being on whom to blame wrongs and accidents.

It will also be remembered that in Protestant countries, although there were no saints with which the slaves could identify their gods, there were more religious practices that seemed familiar to the slaves, especially in the Baptist Church, than there were in Catholicism. The majority of blacks still belong to the Baptist or Methodist churches, and black church services are still generally less formal than white services. Although in some regions one could not tell the difference between a white service and a black service, in other regions, especially in the rural areas of the U. S. South, there is dancing and possession and shouting much as in the past. It is an experience to attend a service at the Methodist church that serves the people of the South Carolina Sea Islands. A slow hymn is begun, and for the first verse there is only singing, but at the beginning of the second verse the congregation begins to clap. As the service proceeds, the clapping increases in speed and intensity, and the African rhythms are unmistakable. All the while, the tempo of the hymn is as slow and its tone is as mournful as when it was begun.

As in slavery times the Catholic Church service is too strict and too rigidly defined for blacks to embroider upon it. Thus, in the Catholic countries of the New World officially sanctioned religious practices, though participated in by blacks, are but one type of religion practiced by them. Other practices, disapproved by the Church, are continued, but they have changed since slavery times.

In Brazil the Batuque has changed, and much more so than other African-influenced religions in the country. For one thing, the Batuque membership is no longer particularly black. Although most members are aware that the religion was once that of dark-skinned descendants of slaves, they are quick to express the belief that "mediums are not chosen by their color." Today, the majority of the Batuque membership is of Brazilian Indian heritage.

As the heritage of the membership has changed, so has the make-up of the pantheon, or group of gods, worshiped. Today the gods are practically all those of the Brazilian Indians or racially mixed people; few of the African gods or African names remain.

The Batuque today also places more emphasis upon individual worship than upon group worship, and thus its rituals and ceremonies are less elaborate. Among more conservative Afro-Brazilian sects—the candomblé groups in Bahia and some of the Xangô groups in Recife—there is much stronger group orientation and much more emphasis upon elaborate ritual. In all of them there remains a strong sense of an original African source, and the members try to continue African religions. The gods have African names and are thought to have permanent residences in Africa.

The Batuque no longer even prescribes rules concerning who can become mediums. In the past, mediums were often the children of other mediums; at least they were people who had been born into the cult. Today, half of Batuque mediums are converts, which is to say they became members of the cult after they had reached adulthood.

Some of these changes may be due to the fact that, during the 1920's, the Brazilian government actively persecuted the Batuque. As perhaps the largest Afro-Brazilian sect and as a sect that traditionally comprised the underprivileged classes, it was seen as urging revolt. Its all-night ceremonies were banned because they were thought to incite the masses. Its curing rituals were seen as black magic rites. Even though that period of persecution ended and the present Brazilian constitution ensures freedom of worship, it would be fairly easy for a hostile government to stop many Batuque activities. Thus, the Batuque has become a more individualized religion, a less foreign religion, a less exclusive religion partly out of necessity.

Even so, with the more African cults, the Batuque has formed a new Federation of Afro-Brazilian Cults. Should the federation gain power, the Batuque mediums might be able to resist interference from local authorities. Perhaps in safer circumstances and with increased contact with cults that continue to be more African in character, the Batuque will change again.

Voodoo has changed as well in the West Indies and in New Orleans, where it was brought by escaped slaves and free blacks who fled the islands during the slave revolts of the early nineteenth century. In Haiti, where voodoo saw its greatest expression in the New World, the practice of voodoo varied according to who was ruling Haiti. In general, the leaders have publicly opposed voodoo. Even Toussaint L'Ouverture, who used voodoo so effectively in inciting the slaves to revolt and to win control of the island, waged war against the cult after he came to power. All of the early leaders tried to suppress the cult. Undoubtedly, they believed that the voodoo that had unified the slaves against their white masters could produce the same results against them. Nevertheless, while publicly rejecting voodoo, many of these leaders secretly consulted voodoo priests and offered sacrifices to the gods. Also, despite the laws against the cult, voodoo ceremonies were always allowed on national holidays and at religious festivals. Later leaders were against voodoo because they felt it was an obstacle to civilization and because they did not feel the upper classes (who practiced Catholicism) should have a different religion from that of the lower classes (who practiced a mixture of Catholicism and voodoo). But voodoo persisted.

During World War I and for several years afterward, Haiti was under American occupation, and the military officials enforced the antivoodoo laws strictly. Temples were destroyed, priests were sentenced to hard labor on public works or given heavy fines. For a time it seemed that voodoo would disappear. But later the American marines began to take an interest in the cult and voodoo flourished again. Later, it was suppressed again. Then, in 1957, François Duvalier, called "Papa Doc," came to power and initiated a dictatorship stronger than Haiti had seen in years. Duvalier effectively shut the island off from the rest of the world and at the same time stressed black nationalism to his subjects. Voodoo enjoyed a resurgence under Papa Doc, and he used voodoo to his great personal advantage, allowing and encouraging his subjects to believe he had *power*. Even if his lower-class subjects were unhappy, few would dare protest against the government, due to the danger of having some evil curse put upon them. He was not called Papa Doc for nothing.

In Haiti, as in Brazil, the state religion, Catholicism, is not enough for the peasants. Christianity is practiced—on Sundays, at baptisms, marriages and deaths—but the familiar daily religion is voodoo. It will be remembered that the slaves incorporated Christian elements into their religion, and today there are many such elements in voodoo. God is recognized as the Supreme Being, the Creator of man and of the world. In the opening rituals of voodoo ceremonies the prayers are Catholic and are often accompanied by the sign of the cross. Many of the original African deities as well as those that have been created in Haiti have Christian counterparts in the Catholic saints. But God and even the saints are considered too remote to care about individual people.

More important, today as in slavery times, are the
loas, who occupy a position between the higher gods
and man, and who are concerned with individual
man's problems. Some of the loas are African deities
who have been passed down through the generations.
Others are powerful ancestors. Some people believe
that the saints are loas, although not all loas are
saints. Each person has one or more loas who are
important to him, but he has one chief loa-protector.
Each loa insists upon certain taboos, or things which
his followers must not do, and upon certain honors,
such as offerings and ceremonies and sacrifices. If a
worshiper observes the taboos and properly honors
his loas, they will help him. If he does not, they will
punish him. The members of a cult strive to please
the loas by providing the proper food, drink, songs
and dances and by wearing the proper clothing at the
various ceremonies. They also avoid breaking the
taboos. Loas are believed to frequent springs and
trees and other natural areas. Thus, followers avoid
throwing garbage near streams, lying under sacred
trees, or tying a horse near one of these spots. Since
the loas sometimes make themselves known to their
followers outside of the regular ceremonies, faithful
worshipers keep themselves pure and in a proper
condition to receive their messages on sacred days.
Some Haitians believe that there are certain loas
who are bad no matter how much they are honored.

Haitian voodoo places great importance upon the
dead. All the dead are called *zombies*, but the term
zombies is used for a special class of the dead. These

are persons who were killed by sorcerers, who have died in accidents or in other unhappy ways, and who have been resurrected by evil priests who use them for evil purposes. There are many other classes of the dead—children who died before baptism, dead twins, people who were changed into animals by sorcerers, people who feel they were neglected and who return to persecute their relatives.

The majority of the dead, of course, die of natural causes. Haitian peasants believe that the spirits of all these dead return to God to receive their reward or punishment. Some good souls remain in the sky with God, others return to earth as good loas, and still other good souls are inherited by newborn babies in future generations. Bad souls become bad loas and return to do evil on earth. It is very important that the dead be honored with elaborate wakes and funeral rites, numerous prayers, Catholic Masses and voodoo ceremonies in their honor. It is also very important that all the dead be included in any voodoo service.

Voodoo services are not the demon-worshiping rites and mad orgies that they once were, although they contain some traditional elements. The rites were never written down, but were handed on by word of mouth from generation to generation, and thus they have changed greatly, with many Christian practices added over the years. They are usually in two parts—a service, which only family and priests attend, and a dance, to which others are invited. Ceremonies take place inside, in temples with altars separated by curtains. Various sacred objects are placed on the altars, and sacrificial animals are placed in front of them. The sacred objects include ceremonial drums, a large knife or sword, a beaded rattle, a bell, an earthenware jug, an egg, candles and a bottle of loa perfume. The sacrificial animals are usually cocks, although a male pig or goat and sometimes a bull may be used in certain rites. The meat of the sacrificial animals is cooked and eaten by the worshipers after a small portion is offered to and "accepted" by the loas.

The high priest is called a *houngan* and is usually a man. In some sections priestesses, or *mambos*, preside. Before starting the actual service there are prayers, usually Catholic, and hymns. Then there is an invocation, or calling, to Legba, the most revered deity, followed by the welcoming of the arriving loa. Each of the loas has a special color, which is used on its special flag. The flags are waved periodically throughout the service. The welcoming of the loa is called the Salute to the Flag, and it is one of the most important rituals. The service is very solemn and very religious.

Then comes the dance, to which friends and neighbors are invited. It is a festive occasion. Although liquor may be offered to the guests as well as to the more important members of the family, the dance never becomes a drunken, frenzied orgy. The drums and rattles set up the rhythm for the songs of the loas, and the chanting of the songs is accompanied by dances to the loas. The arrival of each loa is shown by the behavior of certain worshipers, called *serviteurs*, who become possessed, or "ridden." This is the high point of the service, for possession is proof that the loas have seen fit to come to the ceremony. The possessed are sometimes able to transmit messages from the loas, although that is usually the function of the houngans.

Although the voodoo ceremonies remain important in Haiti, more common and more lasting are the everyday acts and magical beliefs. A peasant child learns early to be aware of his acts, the simplest of which can have great meaning. He learns to be wary of neighbors, for he finds that his elders suspect them of causing some of the family's misfortunes. Sicknesses, deaths, and crop failures are almost as likely to be due to jealous neighbors as to the loas or the dead. While it is not usual for a family to call upon the gods during a regular voodoo service to punish its enemies, a person might ask a loa privately for help in getting back at an evil neighbor. As most of the superstitions and beliefs of Haitian voodoo can be found in New Orleans voodoo and in American Negro hoodoo, they will be discussed in these sections.

Although over the generations Haitian voodoo practices have changed and become milder, Haiti, because of its predominantly black population, because of its long independence and its isolation, especially in the last twenty to thirty years has retained more Africanisms than other black communities in the New World. Voodoo in Haiti remains the purest form of New World voodooism.

New Orleans has not known such conditions as Haiti, and thus the voodoo tradition has changed considerably there. It still exists, but in a much milder and less African form. That it remained such a strong tradition until after the Civil War is due chiefly to Marie Laveau, or rather to the Marie Laveaus, Marie I and her daughter. It will be remembered that a woman named Marie Laveau became the most important voodoo queen in New Orleans in the 1830's. So great was her reputed power and so popular did she become that all the other voodoo leaders and their cults came to look to her for ultimate leadership. This was very fortunate for the practice of voodoo in New Orleans, for under Marie Laveau voodoo became "centralized" and thus very strong. More will be told about Marie Laveau in the next chapter, but it is important to mention here that as she grew older she apparently did not wish to relinquish her power. What she did to prevent this was to groom her daughter, also named Marie, quietly to take over her duties. Although it seems a little hard to believe, the transition seems to have been made so smoothly that most people did not even realize that a substitution had been made. Instead, legends arose that Marie Laveau was ageless, practically immortal. When the newspapers announced in 1881 that Marie Laveau was dead, most people believed that the incredibly young-looking queen of the voodoos whom they had seen walking the streets had died. They did not realize she had looked nearly a century old when she died.

When Marie I became too old, it was Marie's daughter who reigned as voodoo queen. Under the tutelage of her mother, she tried to continue all the traditional voodoo practices, but change is inevitable, and things passed down from generation to generation invariably become altered, just as a rumor is changed as it is told by one person to another, and by that person to another, and so on. In the late 1950's an old black woman recalled:

"Marie Laveau used to call St. Peter something like 'Laba.' She called St. Michael 'Daniel Blanc,' and St. Anthony 'You Sue.' There was another one she called 'On Za Tier;' I think that was St. Paul. I never did know where them names come from. They sounded Chinee to me."[12]

Other Catholic elements continued to be mixed with the voodoo rites. Ceremonies began with the reciting of the Apostles' Creed, which was followed by prayers to the Virgin Mary. A statue of the Virgin generally stood upon the altar.

Marie II also continued her mother's tradition of dispensing gris-gris, particularly love charms. The Laveaus were famous for their love charms, and probably love brought more people to their cottage than anything else.

In love charms, as well as other charms, the principle of "like to like" was applied whenever possible. A young girl would be told to bring the glove of the man she loved. This would be filled with a mixture of steel dust, sugar and honey. The sugar and honey were to "sweeten" the man, the steel dust was for *power*. The girl was told to sleep with the glove under her mattress and she would gain the man's affection.

If a woman wanted a married man, the Laveaus' procedure was to write the name of the man and his wife on a piece of paper, place the paper in an animal bladder fresh from a slaughterhouse, and hang it in the sun to dry. The charm would cause the man to leave his wife. Of course then the woman would need other charms to make him her own, but she could do so with love powders and oils.

Often, parents would ask Marie Laveau to prevent their daughter or son from marrying a person of whom they did not approve. One of the favorite charms for breaking up such a romance was a mixture of gunpowder, mud from a wasp nest, flaxseed, cayenne pepper, BB shot, filé, bluestone and dragon's blood. The mixture was thrown on the front steps of the undesirable person's house.

Marie II is also said to have continued the traditional rites of animal sacrifice and the drinking of blood, usually that of a black cat.

But when the newspapers announced in June 1881 that Marie Laveau was dead, much of Marie II's power was destroyed. Although she reigned still as the queen of the voodoos, other female voodoo leaders now challenged her position. Voodoo in New Orleans split into many parts, and more leaders arose than there had been before Marie I had bound them together under her powerful direction. One

Malvina Latour tried to take the Laveaus' place, but she did not succeed. It is possible that one reason why she did not succeed was that she tried to remove Catholicism and all Catholic practices from voodoo. Although she was a Catholic herself, she considered voodoo a profession and felt that the incorporation of Catholic practices into voodoo was sacrilegious. By the 1890's Malvina Latour was not ruling all the voodoos in the city but only the largest and most important sect.

By 1895 city authorities were again launching a full-scale attack upon the voodoos, and it was at this time that voodoo as an organization was actually suppressed. Never again would there exist the centralization that had existed under Marie Laveau, and never again would voodoo leaders have the power they had once enjoyed.

Correspondingly, voodoo practices changed to become more acceptable to the larger society. A very old black named Joe Goodness remembers witnessing voodoo rites when he was young, around the turn of the century:

In my day they didn't even drink blood, that I know of, but only ate things like gumbo and chicken and drank a lot of liquor. In my uncle's day they did worse things. They used to tear chickens to pieces and eat 'em while they was still alive. They wore all kinds of *gris-gris* tied on their bodies—dolls made out of feathers and hair, skins of snakes and pieces of human bone. I heard people say hoodoos was cannibals and used to eat babies, but I don't believe that unless it was 'way back even before my uncle was alive. I guess it changed a lot, just like it's different now from the way it was when I was a little boy.[13]

By the early 1900's the emphasis of voodoo centered upon the use of gris-gris, the placing and removing of curses rather than upon dances and orgies. Yet, some rites continued and were reported in detail in the first two decades of the century. One Numa Luabre was accused of killing cats with his bare hands in 1915, this act accompanying other weird rites.[14] Although the newspapers turned their attention away from voodoo and to the events of World War I, during the late teens and early twenties of the twentieth century here and there a paragraph would appear describing authentic voodoo rites. Authors writing of New Orleans or of black folklore gave detailed descriptions of rites they had witnessed or participated in in the 1920's and 1930's. Even in the 1940's Congo Square was the scene of many strange findings. An early morning stroller in the area might come upon, for example, a rooster tied to a tree. The poor bird would still be alive, but all its feathers would have been plucked and sticking in its breast would be nine silver pins. Another early riser might find a plate of black-eyed peas and rice cooked with sugar, surrounded by silver coins.

Today, despite what some particularly superstitious New Orleanians might lead one to believe, there are no ceremonies or dances out at Lake Pontchartrain or anywhere else. And most other rituals, such as those mentioned above—rituals that might be described as public in character—occur only rarely if at all. It should be mentioned here, though, that in July 1973, some very strange things were reported found in New York City's Central Park. On one occasion it was a chicken's carcass; on another, it was a pig's head. Although to the uninformed, these findings were unexplainable, to those who knew about voodoo, the reports had a very familiar ring. But whether or not these reports indicate voodoo in New York City, voodoo has continued to live in this century.

One indication of the living quality of any religion or cult is the addition of new elements. The Batuque in Brazil could not have remained a vital force without adopting certain gods and practices of the Brazilian Indians. Although voodoo did not change in character as much as the Batuque, it, too, adopted new elements.

In 1921, Mother Leafy Anderson, who was a spiritualist, arrived in New Orleans claiming to be accompanied by the spirit of an Indian chief named Black Hawk. Mother Anderson was not a voodoo; in fact she detested voodoo. The many spiritualist churches she founded in New Orleans had no voodoo elements about them or their practices. But Black Hawk became a voodoo saint, and the reason for this was, of course, practical. Mother Anderson's spiritualism attracted many blacks and poor whites, and, to cash in on some of this popularity, the voodoos adopted the spirit of Black Hawk, adding him to the already large group of beings worshiped by the voodoos. As one voodoo, Madame Cazaunox, put it, "He's new and he's young, and me, I didn't pay him no mind for a long time, but, goddamit, you gotta admit he's sure good when you is in trouble. I tried him lots of times and he sure has got a lot of *power*."[15] True to African tradition, if a spirit or god *works*, you worship him, no matter whose god he is.

As a matter of fact, in the 1920's, not long after Mother Anderson and the spirit of Black Hawk arrived in New Orleans, voodoo enjoyed a certain resurgence. With the end of World War I, the first *world* war and a war that shattered the sense of security of many people, a great wave of spiritualism swept England and America. In groups people held séances, presided over by a medium, in an attempt to reach loved ones who had died in the war. Individually or in pairs, people played with Ouija boards and automatic writing. Although communication with the departed dead was not a particularly important aspect of voodoo, nevertheless voodoo benefited also by renewed interest.

Today, we are experiencing another wave of spiritualism, and voodoo is still around to benefit from it. It is a different voodoo from that originally practiced by black slaves; it is a much more individual cult now, and much tamer than the original version. However, it is still a fascinating part of the black world—and even of the white.

Few of the original voodoo gods are worshiped

or even remembered. The snake god, called Zombi, is spoken of, but more out of habit than real belief. Perhaps this spirit is considered too remote to be useful. St. Marron (or Maron), who, during slavery times, was worshiped as the patron saint of runaway slaves, secms to have been completely forgotten. Obviously, as there is no more slavery, there is no more need for an antislavery saint. Today, Black Hawk is one of the most important saints, but more important than even Black Hawk is St. Expédite. The word *expédite* in French means the same thing as our word, *expedite*, basically, "to make easier." St. Expédite's origin is not known, but he seems to have arisen in this century, or perhaps late in the last. He is a good example of the continued blending of elements of African religion and Catholicism. There are statues of St. Expédite in at least two Catholic churches in New Orleans and there are two St. Expédite spiritualist temples; yet in terms of works St. Expédite is as African or as voodoo as he can be. Many New Orleanians believe St. Expédite is the most dependable saint when it comes to getting things done in a hurry. All one has to say is, "St. Expédite, do this now," and it will be done. Later, the satisfied worshiper visits one of the St. Expédite statues and makes a suitable offering in gratitude. Sometimes this consists of burning a candle and saying a prayer, but a true voodoo always leaves a special token, a slice of poundcake, a new penny or a sprig of green fern at St. Expédite's feet.

Since the Laveaus there has never been a female
voodoo leader who attained their popularity and reputation. There has also never been a female voodoo
leader who was able to reunite all the voodoo cults
to make the strong system that voodoo became under
the Laveaus. However, there have been female voodoo leaders who have been acknowledged queens
and who have claimed the right to the voodoo
throne. Today, the queen of voodoo in New Orleans
is a woman known as Lala, and in his book *Voodoo
in New Orleans,* Robert Tallant has written about
her. Although she is old and insists she used to be
much more evil, the voodoos of New Orleans admit
that her charms have the greatest power. In fact,
she has so many customers that she has to move
three times a year or else she feels she will not have
a moment's peace.

Spirits surround Lala always and she talks to them
as if they were visible and actually there. They are
with her, too, when she holds meetings, which are
quiet, rather tame versions of the once huge and
ritualistic public ceremonies of past voodoo days.
There is not even a snake anymore, which Lala
greatly regrets. She used to use snakes in her rituals
and considers them very important to the ceremony,
but her neighbors reported that she kept a snake
to the police, and the police came and took it to
the zoo. Now, Lala has to work with pigeons and
chickens and ducks. Even so, she considers her
charms, her gris-gris, very powerful. She insists that
she has the spiritual support of Marie Laveau in her

work, and she has read all the books on voodoo and hoodoo.

Lala's charm for making a person go away is to melt a black candle and to knead the wax like dough. Write the person's name on a piece of paper four times frontward and five times backward. Roll the wax into a ball and put the paper in the middle of it. Then stick nine pins in the ball. Then get on the ferryboat and go out to the middle of the river and throw the ball in. Snap your fingers and say, "St. Expédite, make him go quick!" When the person does go away, you are to take a piece of poundcake to the statue of the saint in Our Lady of Guadalupe Church and leave it at its base. Lala says that the saying "I'm on pins and needles today" comes from the voodoo practice of sticking pins into an object representing a person.

Lala often insists she no longer does evil, but she will do evil to someone who is doing evil to her and not consider her action evil at all. When one of her cats was poisoned, she was sure that a man she knew had done it. So she burned a black candle on the man and gave him bronchitis.

There are many other practicers of voodoo, and showing how much voodoo has changed since slavery times is that some one-third of the voodoos practicing today are white.

Blacks in the New World have long understood that a religion or a system of magic works only if there is belief. "Black man's magic isn't white man's magic," the slaves used to say. Over the years, many whites, especially those of the poorer classes, have come to believe, and thus, for them, black man's magic is white man's magic.

Belief in voodoo by whites has probably helped voodoo to stay alive in New Orleans, but the race of the believers is not as important as belief itself. Voodoo leaders like Lala could not remain in business very long if there were not many people who believed in their power. Voodoos would gris-gris each other off very quickly if only voodoos believed in gris-gris. No, voodoo remains alive because many, many people firmly believe in it.

In 1953 a back-country Southern farmer was arrested for the killing of two elderly women. He explained that they had put a "hex" on him. They had threatened to kill him and had made a doll in his image. By sticking pins into the doll, they had caused him serious illness and he had decided to kill them before they killed him. In 1960 a woman was alarmed to find a dead black cat with a cross on its back on her front steps. Old women still hang pictures of their enemies upside down over their bureaus. Some people put offerings in front of Marie Laveau's tomb especially on St. John's Eve, the most important voodoo feast day. Others make crude dolls of feathers bound with string; each day they unwind a bit of the string, firmly believing that when it is all unwound and the feathers fall apart their enemy will die.

Many New Orleanians still faithfully scrub their front stoops with brick dust. Other nail horseshoes or tack Roman Catholic "holy pictures" above their doors. All these actions are done for protection against evil gris-gris. But the most secure method is to make regular purchases from certain voodoos of counter gris-gris, charms to be worn upon the person or kept within the home.

Many New Orleanians are constantly watchful for evil gris-gris, searching their houses and property at regular periods to make sure nothing is hidden beneath the steps or in the flowerpots. Such hidden gris-gris are really evil and are placed only by persons who intend real harm. Most gris-gris, though, are only meant to cause discomfort and are placed in plain view.

Some people are so afraid of being "hoodooed" or "crossed" that they are suspicious of everything. They will look at a group of pebbles and see "an evil arrangement," or a stick and decide that the way it is pointing means something. Such people spend quite a bit of money paying voodoos to "uncross" them. Other people rather enjoy, in a strange way, being crossed. They will cry and moan and enjoy very much being the center of attention in the neighborhood. Some will carry on and build up their own fear so much that they actually will die. Then their families will have a certain distinction for having a member who has been hoodooed to death.

With the renewed interest in witchcraft and the supernatural in America, voodoo has become something of a big business, at least where the sale of voodoo books and charms is concerned. This is true not only in the South but also in the North, where every city with a substantial black population knows about voodoo. After World War I many Southern blacks migrated to the North to look for better jobs and less discrimination, carrying with them their religious and magical traditions. Today, in nearly every major American city one can buy at a "drugstore" or order from a mail-order house such items as Love Powder, Drawing Powder, War Powder, Peace Powder, Controlling Powder, Anger Powder, Bad Luck Water, Lucky Lucky Water, Sacred Sand, Follow Me Drops and many others. One can also buy sacred pictures of various Catholic saints. St. Anthony de Padua stands for luck; St. Mary Magdalene is said to help women who are in love; St. Joseph, holding the infant Jesus, is used to get a job; a picture of the Virgin Mary will prevent illness, and one of St. Peter will bring great and speedy financial success.

Robert Tallant interviewed many black people in studying voodoo in New Orleans, but a hotel waiter seems to have described best the relationship of voodoo to blacks:

". . . voodoo is part of my people. I think they need it. When white people mess with it, that's different. They're just ignorant or they're after something—like white gamblers will always carry lodestones, or most of them, anyway—but with my race it's something else; it's something to turn to when they're in trouble and it's something to use to get even with people who have done them harm.

Of course maybe I just say this because I know more about my race. Maybe it's the same whether they're white or black . . . And it ain't only in New Orleans. I've been all over the country and I've seen signs of Voodoo almost everywhere, anywhere people of my race live. You can always find it. Of course lots of white people don't know anything about it, but we always know. Anywhere they go my people know the signs."[16]

MAGIC IN THE BLACK WORLD

Although the term "hoodoo" was originally just some American's mistaken pronunciation of voodoo, and although the words *voodoo* and *hoodoo* are often used interchangeably, there is a difference. While voodoo has become chiefly a magical system, there is still some religious meaning embodied in the term, and in this country it is still seen as centered in the New Orleans area. Hoodoo does not have any real religious meanings connected with it, and one rarely hears a reference to a hoodoo "cult." While voodoo is associated with French-speaking areas, hoodoo is more often seen as a strictly American Negro system, based, of course, upon voodoo, but with a quality all its own. The chief reason is that while the large influx of refugees from Haiti and Santo Domingo into New Orleans around 1800 also brought with it a large number of practicers of voodoo who settled in or near the city, no such large group ever reached other parts of the U. S. South. In these other parts voodoo was practiced and believed in by only a few people, some here, some there. Carried as it was by smaller groups, it remained less intact and changed more readily. No organized voodoo cult emerged anywhere outside of New Orleans, no voodoo queens like Marie Laveau arose; in fact, in contrast hoodoo is practiced chiefly by men. Newspapers did not romanticize the cult elsewhere. Thus, in other parts of the U. S. South, though voodoo continued, it changed, and became hoodoo.

Hoodoo charms are very much like those of voodoo. To hurt an enemy, one only has to write his name on a piece of paper, put it in a dead bird's mouth, and let the bird dry up. Your enemy will have much bad luck. If a woman wants revenge upon another woman, she gets a bit of her enemy's hair; if she keeps it, all the woman's hair will fall out. To get rid of people, dry three pepper pods in an open oven, then place them in a bottle, fill it with water, and place it under your doorstep for three days. When the three days are up, sprinkle the water around your house, saying "Leave here," and the people will never come back. To win love, take some of the desired one's hair and sleep with it under your pillow.

Hoodoo charms, like the voodoo gris-gris, can be turned against the person who has placed them. This is usually referred to as "turning the trick." Usually, a person who knows a trick is being worked against him does not know how to "turn it." He must seek help from a "conjure doctor."

As in Africa and as in slavery times, there is a definite distinction between one who practices medicine and one who practices magic. The same differences remain, with the added difference that, today, medical practitioners are mostly women, while the practitioners of magic are mostly men. If you are ailing and do not know the cause, you visit an "herb woman"; if you are ailing and suspect someone has laid a "hoodoo" upon you, you visit a "conjure doctor."

There are many fewer conjure doctors than there are medical practitioners, and perhaps one reason is that their duties are far more complex. A conjure doctor is expected to diagnose the case, tell whether the person is being conjured or not, find out who "laid the trick," find the trick and either tell his customer how to destroy it or how to turn it back against the person who laid it. In addition, if he is to be considered a real conjurer, he must also be able to lay tricks himself, to locate buried treasure or a vein of water.

"Turning the trick" is, of course, one of the most respected acts in hoodoo, and black folklore is full of stories of successful turnings. One man who studied folklore in the South reported:

Ed Murphy did this by laying the trick he had discovered in a piece of paper, sprinkling quicksilver over it, and setting the paper on fire. The trick exploded and made a hole in the ground a foot deep as it burned up—his enemy soon died. "It is said that if any one tricks you and you discover

the trick and put that into the fire, you burn your
enemy, or if you throw it into the running water
you drown him."[17]

The whole concept of "turning the trick" is a
fine example of the persistence of the African tradition that good and evil can reside in the same
thing. So, for that matter, are the conjure doctor
and his works. For, although he can help a person
who has been conjured or hoodooed, he can also
conjure or hoodoo others. Although he does not
usually call upon the spirits of the dead in working
his conjures, many of the materials and methods
he uses reflect the African tradition, though perhaps not remembered consciously, of the power of
dead ancestors. Graveyard dust, for example, is often
used, being called "goofer dust." It is believed
that ghosts cannot cross water, and thus if a conjure
doctor wants to sic a dead spirit upon a man who
lives across water, he must first hold a mirror ceremony to bring the victim from across the water.
Dirt from sinners' graves is believed to be very
powerful, but some conjure doctors will use only
dirt from the graves of infants. They feel that the
sinner's spirit, which is housed in the dirt of the
grave, is too powerful and too unruly. It will kill
the intended victim, certainly, but then it may
start killing others. Few conjure doctors want to
unleash that kind of power.

Belief in witches and vampires can still be found
among blacks in America, although vampires are

believed to be uncommon nowadays. Still, old blacks will tell stories about how a young girl constantly declined while an old woman got better and better and how an old woman sucked young people's blood while they slept. Or about how a witch had bloodsucking children. Naturally, there are ways to keep such evil creatures from one's house:

Salt sprinkled thoroughly about the house and especially in the fireplace; black pepper or a knife about the person; or matches in the hair, all bring dire perturbation to these umbrageous visitors. . . . Ha'nts, like witches, may also be kept away by planting mustard seed under your doorstep, or by keeping a sifter under your head while asleep. Some say that ghosts will not budge from a foot with fern seed in the hollow, though one informant recommends fern seed or sulphur to keep spirits away.[18]

The whole idea of little people has by now been pretty much relegated to black folklore. In Surinam, Dutch Guiana, mothers still caution their children to beware of the *bakru*, who inhabit the roads, but now this warning is chiefly due to the mothers' need to make the children fear straying too far from home than to any real belief in bakru. It is the same in the American South, where stories of the tar baby are told to both black and white children. People do not fear spirits or supernatural beings. But the persistence of hoodoo shows they do believe in the desire and the power of their neighbors to hurt them.

In addition to hoodoo, the principal form of black folk belief in the United States is "signs." The word "signs" is used to designate a whole body of magical beliefs, from superstitions to omens to small magical practices and taboos. The same sort of distinction can be found in every other part of the New World. Knowledge of signs seems to be a woman's province especially, and many children who are reared in the South or in South America or in the West Indies grow up with the sense that there is much beneath the surface of everyday acts, that there are meanings for practically every action and event. They range from birth to death, from cooking and eating to combing one's hair, from house cleaning to headaches. Some can be traced directly to Africa, others to Europe, still others to the unique person that the New World black has become.

There are many birth "signs." Placing an iron under the bed of a woman in labor is supposed to ease birth pangs—the same belief has been found in Africa. The birth room is not to be swept until sometime after the child is born. It will be remembered that in Africa and among the slaves it was believed that a child's spirit was not very "loyal," and there was a danger of sweeping the child's new and unfamiliar spirit away. Also African is the belief that twins, the child born after twins, children born with teeth, or with a caul, or veil of skin over their faces are particularly special. Of course in Europe, a child born with a caul over his face is also considered special, and to have second sight or the ability to see ghosts. Charles Dickens' David Copperfield was born with one. The people of the South Carolina Sea Islands still follow the African beliefs about measures to be taken against evil spirits believed to cause women to have miscarriages or babies to die in infancy. They believe, for instance, that, if such a woman buries on its face the last child who dies, those who come after will live. They believe also that such a woman can trick the spirits by selling her child to someone else for a tiny price and in that way assure that the child will live.

OTHER BIRTH SUPERSTITIONS A baby born near midnight will be able to see ghosts. Babies born in the full of the moon will be larger than those born at other times. It is not good to give a child the name of a deceased child. If a baby is pretty, it will be ugly when it grows up; if it is ugly, it will grow up cute.

There are also a number of baby and child signs: Never step over a baby less than a year old, as this stunts its growth. If a child's fingernails are cut before he is one year old, he will be a thief. If a child's nails are cut under a fig tree or rosebush, he will be a singer. If a baby looks in a mirror before he is one year old, he will have trouble teething. (Tie a nutmeg on a string around the baby's neck and that will help.) A baby whose cradle is rocked while it is empty will die. If a baby cries and jumps in his sleep, an evil spirit is bothering him. Playing with keys makes children hardheaded. If a pig gets a baby's tooth, a tusk will grow in the child's mouth; if a dog gets it, the child will have a fang. If a child manages to keep from putting his tongue in the space where a tooth is missing, the new tooth will be a gold one. Vegetable and melon seeds should be planted by a growing child, for they will grow as the child grows. Don't whip the child who burns another; if you do, the burned child will die.

COOKING AND EATING SUPERSTITIONS If you cook cabbage on New Year's, the next year will be prosperous. If someone drops a fork, a hungry woman is coming to visit; if a knife is dropped, a hungry man is coming. If you eat hoppin' John (black-eyed peas and rice cooked together) on New Year's Day, you will have good luck all year. Spilled rice brings good luck. Spilled salt brings bad luck, and, to break the spell, you must throw the spilled salt over your left shoulder and turn around three times. If you sing before making bread, you will cry before it is eaten. If you go to bed without clearing the table, the youngest in the family will not sleep well. (This relates to the African and slave custom of leaving spilled food for the little people and again to the belief that the soul of a young child is not very firmly in residence within him.) To forget to put tea and coffee in the pot is a sure sign that company is coming. If a loaf of bread is upside down on the table, the Devil is around. Don't leave the griddle on the fire after the bread is done; it will make the bread scarce. Don't shake the tablecloth out of doors after sunset, or you will never marry. Don't lend or borrow salt or pepper, as it will break friendship; if you must borrow it, do not pay it back. CLEANING SUPERSTITIONS If you sweep after 6 P.M., you will sweep all your money out of the house. Scrubbing the steps with red brick brings good luck. On Mondays, Wednesdays, and Fridays, wash steps with overnight urine to keep people from "hoo-dooing" you. Burying a dishrag under the steps will cure a wart. If you sweep over a person's foot, he will soon go to jail. If you drop a dishrag, somebody hungry is coming. If you sweep a person's feet he will run off. If you are touched or hit with a broom, always spit on it or you will go to jail. Never sweep dust out of your house after sundown, because you are sweeping someone out of your family. Never wash on New Year's Day or someone in your family will die. A broom can be moved to a new house if the spell is removed from it by passing it through the window of the new house. Never take up ashes at night. Never take ashes out of the room where a person is ill.

SUPERSTITIONS ABOUT THE BODY AND MANNERISMS If your left eye itches, you are going to get a whipping or get into trouble. If your left ear itches, a stranger is coming; if your right ear itches, you will have a disappointment. Never thank someone for fixing your hair or it will fall out. If you worry too much, your hair will turn gray. When combing your hair always throw any loose strands into the fire, lest the birds get it and build a nest and give you a headache. Powdering your face at bedtime will bring good dreams. If your tongue is sore, you have told a lie. If you sneeze in the morning, bad luck is in store for you. If your lips itch, someone is telling lies about you. Nosebleeds are a sign of bad luck. If your left foot itches, you will take an unfortunate journey. If your nostrils itch, it is a sign of company. Sudden or shooting pains in the body are signs of bad luck. If the crown of your head itches, you will soon be passed to a more honorable position. Old blacks do not cut their nails, for they say their strength is in them. Combing the hair at night makes one forgetful. Measuring yourself will cause you to die.

It will be remembered that Africans worshiped thunder gods and that the slaves continued some of the African beliefs. For instance, the slaves were always reluctant to chop a tree that had been struck by lightning, and this can be related to the African belief that anything struck by lightning was claimed by the thunder gods. Today there are still several superstitions about thunder and lightning, although some are closer to European than to African beliefs. In the event of thunder, cover all mirrors, as the reflection may electrocute you. Thunder before seven means rain before eleven. If you burn wood in your house that has been struck by lightning, the lightning will strike your house. When it thunders the eggs won't spoil.

Superstitions and signs about death and the grave

and ghosts have always been abundant among blacks just as they have been abundant among Europeans. Black superstitions about these things today include European beliefs, but some can be traced directly to African beliefs. If a house is haunted, a piece of new lumber should be nailed in a prominent place, for ghosts hate new things. It is a sign of death for a dog to howl. A death in the family can be made known to the bees by jingling keys or beating on a small pan; otherwise, another death will occur within a year. When passing a graveyard, always cross your fingers; if you don't, you will die. If, when you are walking down the street or sitting quietly in the house, you hear a voice calling, don't answer, because it is a sign of death calling. If you plant a cedar tree, you will die when the shadow cast by the tree at noon becomes large enough to cover your grave. If you kill a lizard on a grave, you will die. If a child digs a hole in the yard, he is digging someone's grave. If a dog howls with his head pointing down, it is a sign of death. If you point at a grave, your finger will rot.

There are weather signs and farming signs and hunting superstitions, and so many others that to list them all would take a book in itself. But those given here are enough to show how all-pervasive a belief in higher powers is among many black people. They show how multileveled life can be, and how full one's everyday existence can be when nearly every act has meanings far beyond itself.

The black American supernatural beliefs and practices that have been chiefly covered in this book have been those of Southern blacks, because it has been in the American South that these beliefs have persisted most. But there are manifestations of the black supernatural in the North as well. Many of them seem quite close in some ways to the current white middle-class cults, and it will be found that the members of these Northern black cults tend also to be members of the middle class.

One of the largest is the Gheez Nation in upstate New York. Its members claim kinship with the Falasha, the African Jews of Ethiopia. The Falasha, a people who live in the wild mountain ranges of that country, stuck to their Hebrew faith when the rest of the people turned to Christianity during the fourth century A.D. The Gheez Nation does not seem to practice anything like the religion of the Falasha, however.

The Gheez people are ruled by the strong hand of Empress Mysikitta Fa Senntao, Imperial Ruler of the Gheez Temple, who claims to have come to earth from the sun in order to redeem her people. She speaks often of life on the sun—how pleasant the temperature, how advanced the people, who travel in space ships—but she does not stress a return to the sun. Rather, she stresses bringing people back from the dead and to the peace and joy of the Gheez Nation.

The ceremonies of the Gheez Nation are very impressive, the major portion being dancing in groups so perfectly controlled that professional dancers who have witnessed these groups have marveled at them. Control is very important—the Empress receives her subjects solemnly and they bow to her deeply. Men demonstrate karate exercises in her honor; the women recite poetry expressing their joy at being Gheez.

There are black mediums as well who do not differ in any important way from white mediums. They have important clienteles; they appear on television talk shows.

Thus, the black world of the supernatural runs the gamut from beliefs and practices that are clearly African in character to beliefs and practices that are no different from those of whites, except that their believers and practitioners are black. Even this variety attests to the "staying power" of the black world of the supernatural.

Chapter 5

Three Legendary Figures in the Black World of Witchcraft, Mysticism and Magic

No book on witchcraft, mysticism and magic in the black world would be complete without a discussion of some of its most important figures, legendary and real, past and present. The history of the black world of the supernatural would not have been quite the same without them. Would voodoo in New Orleans have continued as long and as strongly as it did without Marie Laveau? Probably not. What would black folklore and superstition have been like without the mythical figure High John the Conqueror? Probably not nearly as interesting. Nor would the white world of the supernatural have been quite the same if not for people like Tituba of Salem. Together, these figures have contributed much to the living quality of the black world of the supernatural.

MARIE LAVEAU

No one knows exactly when Marie Laveau was born, although it is probable that she was born in New Orleans. Newspaper reporters later wrote that her father had been a wealthy white planter and her mother a mulatto with a strain of Indian blood. Physical descriptions of Marie bear out this reported heritage, for she was said to have curling black hair, Caucasian features, dark skin that had a distinctly reddish cast, and fierce black eyes. The first reliable record of her life is of her marriage to one Jacques Paris on August 4, 1819; both were listed as free persons of color. New Orleans at that time had been an American possession for sixteen years, but it was much more French-Spanish than American. Voodoo was thriving in the city; ceremonies took place frequently out on the shores of Lake Pontchartrain, and the Congo Square dances were held every Sunday. But there is no evidence that the Laveaus were voodoos. Both were Roman Catholics and it is said that Marie was a daily worshiper at the St. Louis Cathedral. Marie's husband was a carpenter, and the couple might well have lived in obscurity for the rest of their lives.

Sometime after their marriage, Jacques Paris disappeared. Although it was reported that he died five or six years after the wedding, Marie had already been calling herself "the Widow Paris" for some time. Faced with having to support herself, Marie began going into wealthy white homes as a hairdresser. She was paid well, but after a while she was not so much interested in the money she was paid as in the information she was able to get. The women confided in her completely, telling things they would not even tell their best friends. About this time she met Dr. John, a voodoo practitioner who specialized in foretelling the future. Dr. John's reputation increased greatly after he began working with Marie Laveau, and no doubt she supplied him with much of the information she heard in the homes in which she worked, making it possible for him to "know" the most intimate details of a person's life.

Sometime in the latter 1820's Marie took a lover named Louis Christophe Duminy de Glapion, to whom she bore fifteen children in rapid succession. Meanwhile, she was becoming head of all New Orleans voodoos. She stopped working with Dr. John, and, shortly after meeting Glapion, she began to become a voodoo queen in her own right. She quickly became a major voodoo leader.

Her rapid rise to fame was due to a number of reasons. For one thing, she was a strong-minded woman, a shrewd and excellent showman, and had a good business sense. At that time there were many voodoo cults and queens, and it did not take Marie long to get rid of most of her rivals. Some were said to have been driven away by Marie's powerful gris-gris, but the majority were disposed of without the use of any supernatural means. When Marie met another voodoo queen on the street, she would simply beat the women until she had promised either to get out of town altogether or to serve Marie.

Marie also increased her power by adding certain new elements to traditional voodoo practices, chiefly Roman Catholic statues of saints, prayers, incense and holy water. These new elements increased the range of people to whom voodoo would appeal, particularly Roman Catholics. Marie Laveau's meetings out by Lake Pontchartrain were always the largest, for she invited many people who had never before seen the rituals—businessmen, newspaper reporters, figures from the sporting world, even the police! By 1830 Marie Laveau was the acknowledged head of the New Orleans voodoos.

Legends sprang up about her. After she took over leadership of the Congo Square dances, stories of her power over the police spread. There were four gates opening onto the square, each guarded by four policemen on Sundays. But they were never able to keep Marie out. Some said she hypnotized them and caused them to step aside. Others claimed to have seen her make them get down on the ground and bark like dogs. The truth is probably that she knew so much about so many important people in New Orleans (from her hairdresser days) that no one dared bother her for fear that their secrets would be made known. Marie loved the legends and thrived on publicity, which brought many customers to her home seeking gris-gris.

About 1830 Marie moved into a small cottage on St. Ann Street, where she was to live until her death. It was from this home that she worked her most powerful and most legendary gris-gris, and it is known that she got the cottage through gris-gris as well. A young man of a wealthy and prominent family was arrested for a crime, and as his trial approached the evidence seemed very strong against him. In despair, his father sought Marie's help, promising to reward her handsomely if she were able to obtain the release of his son. At dawn on the day of the trial Marie entered the St. Louis Cathedral and knelt at the altar for several hours, holding three Guinea peppers in her mouth. Then she rose, secretly entered the courthouse, and placed the three peppers under the judge's chair. The young man was set free by the court, and the grateful father presented the cottage on St. Ann Street to Marie.

The combination of gris-gris—the Guinea peppers in her mouth and prayer at the cathedral—was typical of the Laveau practices, which were often a strange combination of Catholicism and voodooism.

The Laveau practices were *powerful* ones. The little St. Ann Street cottage was filled with clients day and night. Her control over the Negroes of New Orleans was extensive, and it is said that she had the allegiance of every black servant in the city. One way in which she achieved this loyalty was to demand as payment that the servant become her spy for placing or removing a curse or for telling a fortune. With the information she learned in this way, added to the information she herself had gotten in her hairdressing days, she became a renowned fortuneteller for the rich. Thus, she controlled a number of New Orleans whites as well.

Although her major work was with gris-gris and telling fortunes, Marie presided over all major voodoo ceremonies as well as private ceremonies at her home. Police and politicians were not invited to these rituals, which were held every Friday night. These were true snake rituals. A white sheet would be spread on the ground in the yard behind her house and surrounded by lighted candles. Men and women would dance naked on the sheet, in and out among the candles. Marie, fully clothed, would stand in the center, directing the movements of the dancers. Then she would call her snake, and wrap it around her shoulders and do an eerie, twisting, snakelike dance. The other dancers would reach a frenzy and fall down, exhausted.

There were other activities as well. She built a house in another part of the city, right near a body of water and surrounded by bushes so it could hardly be seen from the road. It was whitewashed and became known as the "Maison Blanche," or White

House. It seems to have been only here that Marie allowed the types of ceremonies that had been brought by the refugees from Santo Domingo. Only here was the Devil, Papa La Bas, worshiped; only here did the worshipers eat raw meat and drink the blood of freshly slaughtered animals and fowl. The snake was used here, and the breast was torn from a living chicken and presented to the queen. Marie very wisely understood the value of being "different Maries" to different groups of her followers.

By the 1850's voodoo was at its height in New Orleans, and Marie Laveau was its heart. Glapion had died in 1835, but Marie had long since ceased to depend upon him for her strength. Early in the 1850's she seems to have found a new kind of strength. She became very interested in prisoners, and her visits to the prison, particularly to the cells of condemned men, became frequent. Rarely was she able to save these prisoners from death, but she eased their waiting periods in many ways. She carried on these activities in addition to presiding with a strong hand over the entire New Orleans voodoo cult.

By the late 1860's Marie was old, past seventy, and in 1869 the cult held a meeting and decided she should retire. She presided over her last major ceremony in that year. She seems to have accepted the cult's decision without resentment, for in reality it meant only that she would no longer reign as queen over the dances and ceremonies. She continued her work at the St. Ann Street cottage, and thousands still sought her help. She also continued her work with condemned prisoners.

Then, in 1875, Marie suddenly stopped going to the prison. In fact, she stopped going anywhere. For six years she did not leave the St. Ann Street cottage; only with her death did she leave. But during those six years a younger Marie Laveau, who also lived in the St. Ann Street cottage, walked the streets of the city. She had begun to appear some years before, and to lead certain voodoo rites, but the transition was so smooth that many did not realize a substitution had been made; they merely marveled at how young Marie remained.

The younger Marie had been born in 1827 to Marie and Christophe Glapion. There was a remarkable resemblance between mother and daughter, and perhaps this was one reason why she was chosen among all the other children born to Marie and Glapion. She stepped into her mother's part completely, carrying on most of the same activities, inspiring similar legends. By her time, the name Marie Laveau was so revered that she was considered a queen over the queens, too lofty to preside over public rituals, which were delegated to queens under her. The second Marie Laveau does not seem to have taken the same interest in prisoners as her mother had, she charged higher prices for her gris-gris, and she is said by some to have been meaner. The second Marie never married. Yet in most ways she was her mother reincarnated, and in fact it can be said that Marie the second really never had a life of her own, as her own person.

In 1881 the newspapers announced that Marie Laveau was dead. This was the first Marie. Immediately the most fantastic legends about her death arose—of thunder and lightning ripping through the St. Ann Street cottage, of shrieks of joy from the fiends of hell. Actually, she died peacefully in her sleep, and she died having renounced completely all her previous voodoo connections.

The announcement of Marie Laveau's death dealt a serious blow to the activities of Marie the second. Apparently, other members of the family, who had been eager to erase the connection between voodoo and the family name, realized how the death stories would weaken her power and refused to allow her to continue her practice from the St. Ann Street cottage. Gradually, her influence faded away, and so did she. No one knows what happened to her.

But if the Laveau or Glapion family had thought they could clear the family name of its voodoo connections, they were sadly mistaken, for the legends about Marie Laveau continued and grew. Today the gris-gris made or sold are the same gris-gris Marie used. The tomb of Marie Laveau in St. Louis Cemetery is a revered spot visited by thousands each year. Today, nearly one hundred years after it was announced that Marie Laveau was dead, her name has become synonymous with the word *voodoo*.

HIGH JOHN THE CONQUEROR

High John the Conqueror is a wonderful figure. He is as well known in Southern black folklore as

Br'er Rabbit and the Tar Baby, and he is better loved. High John the Conqueror was the "hope bringer" for black slaves.

He arose fairly early in slavery times, although late enough so that he is a completely black American figure with no African traditions attached to him. He arose in response to the sorrowful conditions of slavery, in response to the sadness and the complete despair of the slaves. They needed hope, they needed to laugh, they needed to sing, and thus they invented a mythical figure to bring them hope and laughter and song.

"First off, he was a whisper, a will to hope, a wish to find something worthy of laughter and song. Then the whisper put on flesh. His footsteps sounded across the world in a low but musical rhythm as if the world he walked on was a singing-drum. The black folks had an irresistible impulse to laugh. High John de Conquer was a man in full, and had come to live and work on the plantations, and all the slave folks knew him in the flesh."[19]

He had come to live and work on the plantations; the slaves could feel his presence. And he was known to be nearest when the work was hardest and the whites were cruelest. Knowing he was near enabled the slaves to laugh and to sing, and the white masters could not understand how they could do so because they did not feel the presence of High John the Conqueror.

He had come from Africa, that was agreed. What he looked like varied from people to people. Some thought he was a great big man. Others thought he was small and low-built. But it did not matter what he looked like; what mattered was that he was the hope bringer, the laughter bringer. He could even take people away from the plantations without their ever being missed.

Sometimes when the work got too hard and the slaves were wishing they could be anywhere but where they were, High John would hear their wishes and go to them. He would suggest that they take a journey, and when some of the slaves expressed fear of the master, John would explain that the master need never know. "Just leave your old work-tired bodies around for him to look at," John would say, "and he'll never realize you're way off somewhere, going about your business." Then he would go off and find a giant black crow, big enough to carry all the slaves on the plantation plus John himself, and together they would go off to many wonderful adventures. They would visit hell and they would visit heaven, and make all the stops in between. Then the huge crow would carry them back to the plantation, and they would resume their work with a song, and the master would never even know they had been gone.

Sometimes John, in his man-shape, would get into trouble with a master. When he did, he usually managed to avoid a licking by doing something that made even the master laugh. Once in a while, though, the master would win out, but even that was no tragedy. "When Old Massa won, the thing ended in a laugh just the same. Laughter at the expense of the slave, but laughter right on. A sort of recognition that life is not one-sided. A sense of humor that said, 'We are just as ridiculous as anybody else. We can be wrong, too.'" The tradition of African realism can be found in the legends of High John the Conqueror too.

While blacks were slaves, High John the Conqueror gave them a kind of freedom. When the Emancipation came, he went away. He did not have to bring his people laughter and song anymore, for now they had their own, through freedom. "High John knew that that was the way it would be, so he could retire with his secret smile into the soil of the South and wait."

High John the Conqueror no longer walks the fields and plantations. He no longer summons huge black crows to take his people away from their daily drudgery. But he lives on, and he is remembered. Many Southern blacks carry the root of the plant in which he is said to have taken up his secret dwelling, a weed called "Johnny the Conqueror." Some consider it a powerful charm for good things —for good luck or to win love. Others put perfume on it and keep it on their person, or in some secret place in their house. "It is there to help them overcome things they feel that they could not beat otherwise, and to bring them the laugh of the day. John will never forsake the weak and the helpless, nor fail to bring hope to the hopeless. That is what they believe, and so they do not worry. They go on and laugh and sing. Things are bound to come out right tomorrow. That is the secret of Negro song and laughter."[20]

TITUBA

The most infamous witch hunt in American history —the Salem, Massachusetts, witch hunt—was touched off by a black woman. Tituba was not a witch and did not consider herself a witch, and thus some might say that she does not belong in this volume, since the Salem witch trials definitely belong in the white world of the supernatural. But Tituba does belong here. Her own customs and beliefs, rooted in Africa, contributed in no small way to the fear that caused the witch hunts, and it is just possible that her understanding of whites, which has often been important in black witchcraft in the New World, went far in helping to save her from the fate that so many of the accused witches of Salem suffered.

Tituba was born and grew to adulthood in Barbados in the British West Indies. She married a fellow slave named John. When the two had been married about ten years, they were both sold to a Reverend Samuel Parris, a New England man who had left his studies for the ministry in order to become a merchant in Barbados. The Reverend Parris's ventures failed in Barbados and at length he decided to return both to the ministry and to

New England. Eventually, he settled in Salem, Massachusetts, with his ailing wife, his daughter Betsy, his orphan niece Abigail, and Tituba and John, to whom he gave the last name *Indian* because he felt everyone should have a last name.

Salem was a cold, gray, unhappy place compared to the sunny warmth of Barbados, and Tituba was very unhappy there. At night she dreamed of returning to her island home, and in her dreams she did so. As the lonely, cold winter set in and the children could not go outside, she found herself describing Barbados to them so that, in a way, they could return there too. During the long winter, these stories became a high point in the girls' lives, and after a while several other young girls were coming to hear them, too.

Betsy, the Reverend Parris's daughter, was about seven years old. She was frail and sickly and given to staring off into space and forgetting to answer when someone spoke to her. Once, when Tituba was telling Betsy, Abigail and some of their friends about Barbados, Betsy actually went into a trance. The others were both excited and frightened—how was Betsy able to fall asleep, or go into a trance, simply from staring at something too long? At first it was thought that Betsy was suffering from a strange illness, but when local doctors failed to diagnose it, the town decided that the "evil hand" was on her, that she had been bewitched. Then her cousin, Abigail, caught the sickness.

They would sit motionless, their eyes glassy, staring at nothing. Sometimes, without warning, they would break into wild shouts and speak gibberish. Abigail would at times yelp like a dog and run about on all fours. Then another young girl caught the sickness, then another, and another.

What was this strange sickness? It would take a psychiatrist to explain it. Partly, it was due to their upbringing. Life in Puritan New England was rigid and bleak. Children were rarely allowed to laugh or play; their lives were limited to school, doing chores and going to church. The bleakest lives were usually lived by the children of ministers and by those young people who were orphans and who were the "bound" boys or girls who worked for Salem families. It was not just a coincidence that the bewitched girls were almost all either ministers' children or bound girls. Betsy's trances had excited the attention and concern of adults who usually could not be bothered with children. Unconsciously, the other girls probably developed similar symptoms in order to attract some attention and concern too. Then, to continue receiving this attention, they invented new and stranger behavior.

At length, the town was convinced that the girls were possessed by the Devil himself. Some way had to be found to free them. Tituba was very worried about how the girls were behaving, although she suspected they were more aware of what they were doing when they had their "fits" than they admitted. When Mary Sibley, one of the town's women, suggested that a "witch cake" be made in order to drive the evil ones from cover, it was Tituba who agreed to do it. The bewitched girls were gathered together at the Parris house, while the Reverend Parris was away, and as Mary Sibley instructed them, Tituba and her husband, John Indian, made the witch cake. According to records from the trials which followed:

A few days before this Solemn day of Prayer, Mr. Parris' Indian Man and Woman made a Cake of Rye Meal, with the Children's Water, and Baked it in the Ashes, and as is said, gave it to the Dog; this was done as a means to Discover Witchcraft, soon after which those ill affected or afflicted Persons named several that they said they saw, then in their Fits, afflicting them.[21]

According to Mary Sibley's instructions, the chimney had been blocked while the cake was baking, and the room had filled with smoke. At length, Tituba had been forced to leave the house to get fresh air. Outside she met an old beggar woman and another woman who had come for some of Tituba's medicinal tea. Tituba re-entered the house with the two women, and immediately the girls cried that it was these three who were the witches. Mary Sibley had told them that the first three persons to enter the house after the dog had eaten the witch cake would be the evil ones. Tituba protested that she was simply re-entering her own home, but the girls answered by going into their fits. Trying to quiet them, she laid her hands upon them, and immediately they relaxed. This seemed to witnesses even further proof that Tituba was a witch. Tituba could not understand her strange power herself. Shortly thereafter Tituba and the other two women were taken off to jail in Boston to await trial.

One would think that with three witches identified the furor in the town would have died down, but quite the opposite happened. Instead of being released from their "spells," the girls seemed to become worse, their fits to increase in intensity. Now they identified other women, and some men, in the town as afflicting them, and soon the prison in Boston was filled with accused witches awaiting trial. Tituba meanwhile had gone through numerous questioning sessions. Although she knew she was not a witch, her questioners were sure she was, and she began to realize that they seemed more kindly disposed to her when she admitted to, or at least did not too strongly deny, their accusations. She realized that in their hysteria the people of Salem could turn upon her at any moment, but she had reason to hope they would not. What began to worry her most as the weeks passed was the new turn the girls' stories were taking. They had begun to speak of a tall black man, some called him an Indian, who directed the witches in their evil works. Tituba's husband, John Indian, was a tall black man, and she became frightened that people would make a connection between him and the stories. She begged him to act bewitched himself, for in this way he would not be a suspect. Although John Indian was reluctant to do what his wife asked, eventually he did as she wished. He bounded up and down like a dog, writhed and twisted on the floor, and did everything else that the girls did. Thus he was safe.

Months passed. In prison, Tituba saw more and more men and women of Salem arrested and brought to trial. She heard of this one and that one being hanged for witchcraft. The two women who had been accused with her were hanged. Still, Tituba remained in jail. About a year after her arrest there was a sudden revulsion in Salem against the witch hunts. Too much blood had been shed, too much hysteria had reigned. The town was exhausted and eager to get back to normal. No new arrests were made, and one by one the people in the Boston prison who had been arrested as witches paid their sixpence-a-day prison fees and were released. Tituba stayed. The Reverend Parris did not want to pay her fees. For a time she wondered if she would ever be free again.

Then a Boston weaver bought Tituba for the price of her fees and shortly after bought John Indian from the Reverend Parris.

Of the twoscore people who had been hanged during the Salem witch hunt, not one was black, and it is due to Tituba's cleverness that neither she nor her husband met the horrible fate suffered by the others.

Footnotes

[1] John Godwin, *Occult America* (Garden City, N.Y.: Doubleday & Co., Inc., 1972), p. xv.

[2] Saunders Redding, *They Came in Chains* (Philadelphia: J. B. Lippincott Co., 1950), pp. 12–13.

[3] Frederika Bremer, *The Homes of the New World*, Vol. 2 (1868), p. 338; Melville J. Herskovits, *The Myth of the Negro Past* (Boston: Beacon Press, 1958), p. 105.

[4] Newbell N. Puckett, *Folk Beliefs of the Southern Negro* (Chapel Hill, N.C.: University of North Carolina Press, 1926), p. 284.

[5] Gayraud S. Wilmore, *Black Religion and Black Radicalism: An Examination of the Black Experience in Religion* (Garden City, N.Y.: Doubleday & Co., Inc., 1972), p. 65.

[6] Bremer, p. 331f; Herskovits, p. 95.

[7] John B. Cade, "Out of the Mouths of Ex-Slaves," *Journal of Negro History*, Vol. 20 (1935), p. 33.

[8] Puckett, p. 394.

[9] E. Franklin Frazier, "The Negro Slave Family," *Journal of Negro History*, Vol. 15 (1930), p. 216.

[10] Puckett, p. 548.

[11] Louis Pendleton, "Negro Folk-Lore and Witchcraft in the South," *Journal of American Folk-Lore*, Vol. 3 (1890), p. 201f.

[12] Robert Tallant, *Voodoo in New Orleans* (New York: Collier Books, 1962), p. 111.

[13] Ibid., p. 26.

[14] Ibid., p. 168.

[15] Ibid., p. 175.

[16] Ibid., pp. 251–52.

[17] Puckett, p. 296.

[18] Ibid., p. 143f.

[19] Langston Hughes and Arna Bontemps, eds. *Book of Negro Folklore* (New York: Dodd, Mead & Co., 1958), p. 93.

[20] Ibid., p. 102. Most of the previous section is indebted to Zora Neale Hurston.

[21] Robert Lucas, "The First Witch of the First Witch Hunt," *Negro Digest*, January 1951, pp. 87–91.

Bibliography

Bradley, Wilbert. "Voodoo in Haiti," *West Indian Review*, August 25, 1951, pp. 15–19.

Bremer, Frederika. *The Homes of the New World*, 2 vols., 1868.

Brewer, J. Mason. *American Negro Folklore*. Chicago: Quadrangle Books, 1968.

Cade, John B. "Out of the Mouths of Ex-Slaves," *Journal of Negro History*, Vol. 20 (1935), pp. 294–337.

Campbell, Joseph. *The Masks of God: Primitive Mythology*. New York: The Viking Press, 1971.

Clayton, Edward T. "The Truth About Voodoo," *Ebony*, April 1951, pp. 54–61.

Coughlan, Robert. "Black Magic: Vital Force," *Life*, April 21, 1961, pp. 118–32.

"Does Black Magic Really Work?" *Jet*, May 20, 1954, pp. 16–17.

"Does Voodoo Really Work?" *Jet*, May 21, 1953, pp. 22–23.

Dorson, Richard, ed. *African Folklore*. Garden City, N.Y.: Doubleday Anchor Books, 1972.

Frazier, E. Franklin. "The Negro Slave Family," *Journal of Negro History*, Vol. 15 (1930), pp. 198–259.

Gelfand, Michael. "On the Rounds with a Witch Doctor," *New York Times Magazine*, March 14, 1965, pp. 44–45.

Godwin, John. *Occult America*. Garden City, N.Y.: Doubleday & Co., Inc., 1972.

Grosvenor, Verta Mae. "Sir, You Are a Huckleberry Beyond My Persimmon," *Redbook*, April 1973, pp. 102–3.

Haskins, Jim, and Hugh F. Butts, M.D. *The Psychology of Black Language*. New York: Barnes & Noble, 1973.

Herskovits, Melville J. *The Myth of the Negro Past*. Boston: Beacon Press, 1958.

Hill, Douglas, and Pat Williams. *The Supernatural*. New York: Hawthorne Books, 1965.

Hughes, Langston, and Arna Bontemps, eds. *Book of Negro Folklore*. New York: Dodd, Mead & Co., 1958.

Leacock, Seth and Ruth. *Spirits of the Deep: Drums, Mediums and Trance in a Brazilian City*. Garden City, N.Y.: Natural History Press, 1972.

Loughlin, Elmer H. "The Truth About Voodoo," *Natural History*, April 1954, pp. 168–79.

Lucas, Robert. "The First Witch of the First Witch Hunt," *Negro Digest*, January 1951, pp. 87–91.

Middleton, John, ed. *Gods and Rituals: Readings in Religious Beliefs and Practices*. Garden City, N.Y.: The Natural History Press, 1967.

Nadel, S. F. "Witchcraft in Four African Societies: An Essay in Comparison." *American Anthropologist*, January–March 1952, pp. 18–29.

Pendleton, Louis. "Negro Folk-Lore and Witchcraft in the South," *Journal of American Folk-Lore*, Vol. 3 (1890), pp. 201–7.

Petry, Ann. *Tituba of Salem Village*. New York: Thomas Y. Crowell Co., 1964.

Puckett, Newbell N. *Folk Beliefs of the Southern Negro*. Chapel Hill, N.C.: University of North Carolina Press, 1926.

Redding, Saunders. *They Came in Chains*. Philadelphia: J. B. Lippincott Co., 1950.

"Science Finding Logic in Voodoo Medicines," *Jet*, October 20, 1955, p. 27.

Simpson, George Eaton. *The Belief System of Haitian Voodoo*. Reprinted from *American Anthropologist*, January to March 1945.

Tallant, Robert. *Voodoo in New Orleans*. New York: Collier Books, 1962.

Wilmore, Gayraud S. *Black Religion and Black Radicalism: An Examination of the Black Experience in Religion*. New York: Doubleday & Co., Inc., 1972.

Index

James Haskins has taught in elementary and junior high schools, The New School for Social Research, the State University of New York at New Paltz, and is presently at the Experimental College at Staten Island Community College and the Graduate Department of Education at Manhattanville College. He is an educational consultant and the author of numerous articles and books including *Profiles in Black Power*, *Resistance: Profiles in Nonviolence*, *The War and the Protest: Vietnam*, and most recently *Black Manifesto for Education*, *The Psychology of Black Language* with Hugh F. Butts, M.D., and *Pinckney Benton Stewart Pinchback*.